ABOVE / *Hail to the victors!*
Klaus Augenthaler of West
Germany hoists the object of
this grand, month–long quest.
Daniel Motz / MOTZSPORTS

WORLD CUP ITALIA '90

LEFT / Soccer is on everyone's mind in Italy, even away from the stadium pitch, where a Korean youth demonstrates his ball–handling prowess in front of an appreciative, multi-national crowd in Naples. Luigi Baldelli / AC

OPPOSITE / The roots of soccer — calcio — run deep in Italy, woven into a rich culture where such historical gems as the 13th century Santa Maria Novella Cathedral in graceful Florence seem almost commonplace. Massimo Siragusa / AC

PRECEDING PAGES / The World Cup — the globe's most popular sport played for national pride before an audience of billions. Any wonder, then, why the emotional highs are so exhilaratingly high and, as seen in Luis Carlos Perea and his Colombian teammates, the lows are so agonizingly low? David Jacobs / Action Images

PUBLISHER — Commemorative Soccer Publications
Mark J. Hugo

PRODUCTION — Commemorative Publications, USA
Mikko "Mike" Laitinen

Suomen International Publications, Finland
Jouni Palmunoksa

MANAGING EDITOR — Lisa H. Albertson

ASSOCIATE EDITOR — John Robinson, Deseret News

USSF ADMINISTRATION — Alan Rothenberg, President
Keith Walker, Secretary General
Kevin Payne, National Administrator
John Polis, Director of Communications

CAPTIONS — Lee Warnick

PRINTING — Esan Kirjapaino Oy
Lahti, Finland

PAPER — Metsä Serla Oy, Äänekoski Paper Mill
Äänekoski, Finland
Galerie Art 135 g

COLOR SEPARATIONS — Ernest D. Miller
Valley Colour, Provo

TYPESETTING — TypeCenter, Salt Lake City

PHOTO-GRAPHERS — David Jacobs, Action Images / London
Steve Hale, Action Images / London
Jon Van Woerden / Ft. Lauderdale
Daniel Motz, MOTZSPORTS / Glendale
Cynthia Greer / New York
Lehtikuva Oy / Helsinki
Sven Simon (Lehtikuva Oy) / Helsinki
Lucas (Lehtikuva Oy) / Helsinki
Alain Landrain, Press•sports / Molineaux
Agenzia Contrasto (AC) - SABA / New York
   Luigi Baldelli, Silva, Massimo Siragusa,
   Dino Fracchia, Donatello Brogioni,
   Simona Cali Cocuzza, Marco Bruzzo,
   Eligio Paoni, Paolo Siccardi, Luca Musella
Keyvan Antonio Heydari / Miami
ENIT - NY / New York
ENIT - SF / San Francisco

WRITERS — Christopher Davies / Daily Telegraph
Keyvan Antonio Heydari
Ridge Mahoney / Assoc. Editor, Soccer America
John Polis / United States Soccer Federation
John Robinson / Deseret News
Graham Turner

SPECIAL THANKS — Kevin Payne, Garry and Ellen Cole,
John Polis, Tarja Laitinen, Lori Hugo,
Mikko Tuomarila, Tuula Palmunoksa,
Riku Salmenkylä, Teresa C. Jones,
Kari Pelli and our friends at Esa,
Patty Butterfield, Karen Bybee,
Jim Trecker, ENIT-SF, ENIT-NY,
David Jacobs, San Topham,
Keyvan Antonio Heydari

Dear Friends:

June 10, 1990 will be a date long remembered in American soccer annals, for that was the date when the U.S. National Team took the field in Florence, Italy, against Czechoslovakia in the first appearance by America in the World Cup Finals since 1950.

All of us involved with soccer in the U.S. felt enormous pride that day, and subsequently in our team's courageous efforts against Italy and Austria.

The United States Soccer Federation is proud to present Commemorative Soccer Publications' photo journalistic record of World Cup Italia '90. We are sure you will treasure it for years to come, and will turn to it often to rekindle the memories of the glorious month of Italia '90.

Our sights now are set on 1994, when the World Cup comes to America. We know we can count on your support in producing the most spectacular World Cup ever, and in achieving new levels of success for our U.S. National Team!

Yours in Soccer,

Alan Rothenberg
President,
United States Soccer Federation

CONTENTS

Throughout the tournament, players such as Cameroon's Emile M'Bouh (No. 8) and Cyrille Makanaky bristled at referees' frequently inconsistent campaign to control rough play. Never before had the men in black played such a large role in the World Cup — records were easily set for yellow cards, expulsions and penalties. David Jacobs / Action Images

world cups past

PELÉ AND PASSION

P elé . . . Eusebio . . . Bobby Charlton . . . Johan Cruyff . . . Franz Beckenbauer . . . Paolo Rossi . . . Diego Maradona. They are among the more notable figures who have left their marks during the 60–year history of the world's biggest sporting event: The World Cup.

Even before the start of the first tournament in 1930 in Uruguay, the World Cup was developing a history that was and is appropriate for the world's premier sporting event.

Political interference? Absolutely. Controversy? By the ton. Spectacular play? A resounding "Yes."

It took 26 years after the initial planning for the event to even come about. After its formation in 1904, the Fédération Internationale de Football Association (FIFA) boldly proclaimed that it was the only organization authorized to organize soccer's world championship. Much of the rest of the world, including the leading football power of the time, the British — who wouldn't enter the competition until 20 years after its inception — didn't even belong to FIFA.

Details were worked out so that in time the FIFA founders were able to see their dream realized.

It was, though, to have a shaky start. Due to disputes and travel time, none of the top European teams entered and only 13 in all competed in 1930. There were no qualifying rounds. All applicants qualified automatically, regardless of where they were located. That has changed dramatically to where today the top 24 teams are selected to compete via rigorous qualifying standards.

It also became apparent that it doesn't hurt one's chances to be the host country. Uruguay in 1930, Italy in 1934, England in 1966, West Germany in 1974 and Argentina in 1978 all won titles on their own soil.

ABOVE / *A select few athletes become so renowned that their names grow to be synonymous with their sport. This is Pelé — no other name needed — of Brazil, whose individual brilliance elevated his team to three World Cup titles between 1958 and 1970. For those who wonder, his given name is Edson Arantes do Nascimento.* Action Images

OPPOSITE/ *Johan Cruyff of the Netherlands, one of the most dominant players in the "post–Pelé era," led his team to a second-place finish to host West Germany in 1974.* Action Images

Through the politics and controversy has emerged a stage for stardom — individually and nationally.

There has been no greater star than Pelé. From the time he appeared in his first World Cup as a 17–year–old in 1958 in Sweden, he has become the yardstick by which soccer players are measured.

He is to soccer what Babe Ruth was and is to baseball. Ask someone who knows little or nothing about soccer to name a soccer player and the answer will be: Pelé.

His flair and precision on the soccer field have been unsurpassed. He played in four World Cups — 1958, 1962, 1966 and 1970. Brazil won three of them during that 12–year span, a feat that has not been matched.

Because of his greatness, teams took extraordinary measures to keep him away from the action. That tactic got so bad in 1966, where he was fouled repeatedly, that he vowed never to play in the World Cup again. Fortunately for Brazil he changed his mind by 1970 to lead his team to its last world title.

The flair of Pelé has been replaced by a trend toward defense in recent World Cups — this year's being no exception. In fact, the average of 2.21 goals per game in the 1990 World Cup is the worst since the World Cup began in 1930, topping the previous low of 2.54 goals per game in the 1986 World Cup in Mexico City.

Despite disappointment in the trend toward defense and a yearning for the happy—go—lucky days, the World Cup continues to draw a worldwide audience who harbors a passionate love for the game of soccer. It is the common man's game, played on dirt fields, in streets and alleyways, and every four years it takes center stage while the world watches.

1930
HOST: URUGUAY

WINNER: URUGUAY

As expected, the first of anything is quite a challenge and so it was with the inaugural World Cup. Uruguay was awarded the first site because it was the 1924 and 1928 Olympic champion and because it promised to underwrite the expenses of the teams coming from Europe. However, only four European teams — France, Romania, Belgium and Yugoslavia — attended.

The final was a replay of the 1928 Olympics: Uruguay vs Argentina. Brotherly love was not exactly in abundance. Langenus of Belgium, the final's referee, accepted the task only after his life was insured. There was also a dispute on which kind of ball would be used in the final. In a Solomon-like move, it was decided to use the Argentine ball the first half and the Uruguay one the second. After taking a 2–1 halftime lead, the Argentines failed to score in the second half as Uruguay rallied for a 4–2 triumph.

A surprise was the play of the United States, which defeated Belgium and Paraguay before losing to Argentina, 6–1, in the semifinals.

1938
HOST: FRANCE

WINNER: ITALY

Italy showed it could win away from home and Brazil emerged as a power. Argentina, upset that Italy was taking so many of its best players, didn't enter.

Spectacular individual play and extreme physical play highlighted this World Cup.

The Brazil–Poland first–round game has been called one of the greatest in World Cup annals. It featured Brazil's extraordinary center–forward Leonidas, who scored four goals to lead his team to a 6–5 extra–time win. Poland's Ernest Willimowski also had four goals.

Brazil then played Czechoslovakia to a 1–1 tie in a game that resulted in ejections and hospitalizations. Brazil won the replay, 2–1, but faced Italy in the semifinals without Leonidas, who had a knee injury. Italy proved to be more formidable, taking a 2–1 semifinal win and then downing Hungary, 4–2, in the final as both Piola and Colaussi scored two goals.

Word War II would postpone the next World Cup until 12 years later.

1934
HOST: ITALY

WINNER: ITALY

Pressure politics interceded in a big way. Mussolini declared Italy would win, then used a Fascist ruling to help his favorite team do so. He declared that any Italian born abroad of Italian parentage was eligible to play for Italy, which enabled him to have four Argentines on his team. Still, Italy had some tough moments. After disposing of the United States, 7–1, in the first round, the Italians faced a determined Spain with its outstanding goalie, Ricardo Zamora. The two battled to a 1–1 tie and had to play a replay 24 hours later. Spain, battered in the first game, had to use seven reserves for the replay, including a backup for its keeper Zamora. Italy defeated the pesky Spaniards, 1–0.

Czechoslovakia looked like it would win the final, taking a 1–0 lead on a goal by left winger Puc with just 20 minutes left in the game. But then Italy retaliated as Orsi, an Argentine, got one past Czech goalie František Planicka to force the game into extra time. Italy dominated the remainder of the game with center–forward Schiavio scoring the winning goal to give Italy a 2–1 victory.

1950
HOST: BRAZIL

WINNER: URUGUAY

Close to 200,000 people viewed the final between Brazil and Uruguay in the Maracanã Stadium in Rio de Janeiro fully expecting a Brazilian victory. It didn't happen. Despite a powerful, attacking team led by Ademir, Jair, Friaca and Zizinho, the pressure became overwhelming. The governor of Rio reportedly made an impassioned plea on the field just before the game began, crying, "Fifty million Brazilians await your victory!"

And while Brazil took a 1–0 lead on a goal by Friaca, it was Uruguay who emerged victorious, 2–1, on goals by Schiaffino and Ghiggia. Instead of a wild, frenzied celebration by 200,000 people, there was tomb–like silence at game's end.

This World Cup also involved perhaps the biggest upset in World Cup history: the United States' stunning first–round 1–0 victory over England in its first–time appearance in the World Cup. The U.S. players were carried off the field by ecstatic Brazilian fans since England had been expected to battle Brazil for the title. Neither country advanced to the second round.

1954
HOST: SWITZERLAND
WINNER: W. GERMANY

For the second-straight World Cup the heavy favorite wound up losing in the championship game.

Hungary was unbeaten in four years and started the tournament looking like it would stay that way at least through the World Cup. Hungary clobbered Korea, 9-0, and then faced the team it would meet in the title game — West Germany.

West Germany, in effect, conned the Hungarians in the first-round contest, using mainly reserves in a 8-3 loss, hoping to get by the next games and then surprise Hungary with a much stronger team in the finals.

That's exactly what happened.

After spotting Hungary a 2-0 lead, Helmut Rahn scored the tying and winning goals to give the West Germans the 3-2 victory.

This tournament was also noted for Hungary handing Uruguay its first World Cup defeat, 4-2, in the semifinals in a game called by some the greatest in World Cup history, and for the first game to be televised — the June 16 contest between France and Yugoslavia.

1962
HOST: CHILE
WINNER: BRAZIL

The 1962 World Cup demonstrated that Brazil was a powerful force even without its acknowledged star, Pelé, who was sidelined after one-and-a-half games with a pulled muscle.

The play was not as stellar as in '58 and violence on the playing field was too much a factor. Before the competition, an Italian journalist got the locals upset by writing a critical article about their country. Thus, when Italy played Chile, there was as much kicking and fouling as playing. Nationalistic pressure peaked when a Chilean player took a swing at Italy's Maschio, breaking his nose, and the referee expelled two Italians!

With Garrincha and Amarildo leading the way, Brazil defeated Spain and England to set up a semifinal game with Chile. Again, the play was rough with Garrincha being fouled repeatedly. When he retaliated, he was expelled. He had by then, however, scored two goals to lead Brazil past Chile, 4-2.

The final held little drama as Brazil played methodically in a 3-1 victory over Czechoslovakia.

1958
HOST: SWEDEN
WINNER: BRAZIL

Pelé. Young and restless and then some. He elevated football to new heights and popularity and started Brazil on the most impressive run in World Cup football history.

For awhile it looked like the 17-year-old player would have to wait a World Cup before becoming an international star. He didn't play in the first two games. After a lackluster 0-0 tie with England, however, a group of his teammates persuaded coach Vicente Feola to start him the next game against the Soviet Union. That was to be the end of his time on the bench. He was brilliant against the Russians and then in the quarterfinals against Wales, scoring what he reportedly claimed was "the most important goal of my career" in Brazil's 1-0 victory.

He was devastating against France in the semifinals, scoring three goals in Brazil's 5-2 victory. He added two spectacular goals in Brazil's 5-2 victory over Sweden in the championship game.

1966
HOST: ENGLAND
WINNER: ENGLAND

The host country didn't threaten any goalscoring records in its first three games, but then it didn't have to. Though England managed just four goals while reaching the quarterfinals, its defenders didn't allow any.

While England was having trouble scoring, Portugal, with "the new Pelé," Eusebio, wasn't. He scored two goals to lead Portugal over Brazil, 3-1. In the quarterfinal match against surprising North Korea, he scored four to rally Portugal from a 3-0 deficit to a 5-3 win.

But in the semifinals, Eusebio and Portugal ran into England's stellar defense and Bobby Charlton. Charlton scored both goals for his team as England halted Portugal, 2-1.

The final was decided in extra time as Geoff Hurst scored twice to lead England past West Germany, 4-2. Hurst had an earlier goal to become the first player to score three goals in a championship game.

On a negative note, Pelé was fouled so badly in the game with Portugal that he vowed to never play in the World Cup again. Four years later that vow would be forgotten.

1970
HOST: MEXICO
WINNER: BRAZIL

The end of the Pelé era. Pelé, though 30, was still outstanding and exciting. Plus, he had gifted teammates like Jairzinho, Carlos Alberto, Tostão and Gerson. While Brazil was considered questionable defensively, it didn't matter. Its offense was so powerful that it dictated the tempo and, as became apparent, the outcome. After defeating Peru, 4–2, in the quarterfinals and Uruguay, 3–1, in the semifinals, Brazil faced defensive–minded Italy in the finals.

Italy wasn't up to stopping Pelé or his teammates in the championship game, however. Brazil was constantly on the attack, with all four of its goals in the 4–1 title–clinching victory electrifying the crowd.

For winning the world title three times, Brazil was awarded permanent possession of the Jules Rimet Cup, named so in 1946 after Frenchman Jules Rimet, past president and one of the founders of FIFA. Unfortunately, the solid gold cup was stolen in 1983 and Brazilian police suspected that it had been melted down by the thieves. A copy of the original now resides in the federation's office.

1974
HOST: W. GERMANY
WINNER: W. GERMANY

The solid play of the host country and the spectacular play of Johan Cruyff and his Dutch teammates highlighted the 1974 World Cup.

The Netherlands was devastating. The Dutch scored 14 goals while allowing only one going into the final. West Germany, much like England eight years earlier, was doing what it had to do to advance — good defense and timely goals. It was led by Franz Beckenbauer. Beckenbauer and Cruyff were regarded as the two most complete footballers in the post–Pelé era.

The Netherlands started fast in the final. After Cruyff dribbled into the West German penalty area and was fouled, Neeskens scored from the resulting penalty kick and the Netherlands grabbed a 1–0 lead. But instead of continuing to press the attack, the Dutch backed off. The West Germans capitalized, tying the contest on a penalty kick by Paul Breitner and scoring the winning goal later in the half on a kick by Gerd Müller. Müller, who had four goals in the tournament, moved into first place in all–time World Cup scoring with 14.

Though the more aggressive team in the second half, the Dutch were unable to score and handed West Germany the championship.

1978
HOST: ARGENTINA
WINNER: ARGENTINA

Argentina, the birthplace of soccer in South America, finally got to host the World Cup. And the host nation's team certainly gave the host nation's fans what they wanted — a championship.

The stars of 1974 — Franz Beckenbauer and Johan Cruyff — did not return. Cruyff cited personal reasons and Beckenbauer's revolved around his involvement with the New York Cosmos.

Still, the Netherlands was a formidable team without Cruyff, advancing to the finals. The problem was, that just like in 1974, it was facing the host nation in the championship game.

Argentina got outstanding performances from Mario Kempes, Fillol, Galvan and Bertoni in the final. It was Kempes who scored the go–ahead goal in extra time and set up the final goal in Argentina's 3–1 victory over the Netherlands.

A new star was introduced by Italy — 21–year–old Paolo Rossi. His wizardry led the Italians to victories over Argentina, France and Hungary before Italy was eliminated.

1982
HOST: SPAIN
WINNER: ITALY

The number of qualifiers was increased to 24 and the competition spanned nearly a month — June 13 to July 11.

All that did was magnify what was to be an electrifying performance by Paolo Rossi. It gave him time to change from a lackluster performer to a superb one.

Through the first four games, Rossi, who had been a sensation in the 1978 World Cup, was held scoreless. Twice, in fact, he had been benched. But that all changed beginning with the quarterfinal game against Brazil. He scored three times to lead Italy into the semifinals against Poland. In the match against Poland, he scored two goals to place Italy into the championship game against West Germany.

Again, it was Rossi who led the way in the finals, scoring the game's first goal 11 minutes into the second half, which made him the tournament's leading scorer with six. The Italians controlled the rest of the game to take a 3–1 victory and join Brazil as three–time World Cup winners.

ABOVE/ Brazil's 12-year dominance of the World Cup was interrupted in 1966 by Portugal, which physically intimidated Pelé and defeated the Brazilians, 3-1, in Liverpool, England. Here, Portugal's Antonio Simões, extreme left, scores his team's first goal against Brazil. Action Images

BELOW / England won its only World Cup title in 1966, thrilling a hometown Wembley Stadium crowd. English star Jack Charlton stops a shot by a West German attacker during his team's 4-2 victory in the final. Action Images

1986

The world was introduced to perhaps soccer's most controversial star — Argentina's Diego Maradona. The football community had been introduced to him at the 1982 World Cup in Spain and the then 21–year–old gave an indication of what was to come — in a crucial second–round game against Spain, Maradona left the field in disgrace after being ejected for committing a vicious foul.

That incident in 1982, however, would fade in comparison to the one that took place in 1986 — Maradona's "Hand of God" goal, one of the most famous — or infamous — in soccer history.

It occurred during the quarterfinal match with England. Early in the second half of a scoreless game, Maradona and English goalie Peter Shilton leaped to try to get a ball in the penalty area. While Shilton tried to legally use his hands to get the ball clear, Maradona somehow got the ball in the net for a goal. Replays clearly showed that Maradona had illegally punched the ball into the net with his left fist, not his head. Asked to explain the goal, Maradona simply said, it was "the hand of God." As was to be seen in the 1990 World Cup, this was not to be the last time that Maradona would use an illegal part of his body during a match.

"Hand of God" or not, Maradona was brilliant in 1986, outfoxing defenses designed to stop him. He scored both goals in the 2–1 quarterfinal victory over England and both in the 2–0 victory over Belgium in the semifinals. And it was his stunning pass to Jorge Burruchaga with just six minutes left that produced the winning goal in Argentina's 3–2 championship triumph over West Germany. ■

John Robinson

ABOVE (top) / *Brothers Jack (left) and Bobby Charlton lit up English soccer in the 1960s. These days Jack is a hero in another country — Ireland — where he coaches the national team.* Action Images

(bottom) / *Political animosity between nations is often set aside during a worldwide sporting event such as the World Cup. Portuguese great Eusebio poses with players from the Soviet Union following a match.* Action Images

OPPOSITE (top) / *World champions enjoy the spoils of victory for four years. English captain Bobby Moore, carrying the World Cup trophy, is welcomed with his teammates by the Irish national team, forming a "guard of honor" in deference to the 1966 world champions, at an October 1966 exhibition match in Belfast, Northern Ireland.* Action Images

(bottom) / *Paolo Rossi and teammates watch with glee as Rossi's goal sends Italy on its way to a 3–1 victory over West Germany. Rossi was a sensation in the newly expanded tournament, scoring six goals and leading Italy to its third World Cup title in 1982.* Action Images

the road to ITALY

The U.S. Soccer Federation, under the leadership of President Werner Fricker, put together a carefully planned strategy of preparing and qualifying a team for Italia '90 years before the event itself. Not since 1950, a long four decades, had the United States made an appearance in the World Cup. And with the disappointment of the 1986 qualifying round — where the United States was eliminated — still ripe in the minds of U.S. soccer leaders, erasing that memory with a qualification for 1990 was a passionate, messianic goal for everyone in the U.S. National Team Program.

The strategy involved a drastic upgrading in the way the Federation had prepared teams for international competition. Since soccer had little tradition of professionalism in the United States — the result being the absence of any established national professional league — there had to be another way of preparing the team through training, and then giving the squad the tough international seasoning that comes through competitive matches.

Throughout the world, the training ground for World Cup players is with their individual professional clubs. Many professional players are under contract to teams outside of their home country's boundaries. They gain the experience of top–flight competition by contesting for a position throughout the week and by playing on Saturday afternoon. The top players are then called up by the national team coach when it is time to prepare for a major international competition.

It's different in the United States. With no national pro league, the challenge facing the Federation was two–fold: find a way to get the team into training on a regular basis, and make sure that all eligible, highly–qualified American players are free to join the team for the large block of time necessary to get the team ready for major competition.

Fricker, along with Sunil Gulati, chairman of the Federation's International Games Committee, devised a plan by which not only would the players be available to train against international competition, but the Federation would also put these players under contract, paying them a wage to ensure their availability for U.S. National Team duty.

With the seeds of this new plan thoroughly sown by the fall of 1987, the Federation began to move the team, which at the time was under the direction of coach Lothar Osiander, into regular international competition. Trips to Central America, the Far East and Europe, as well as a barrage of matches against top international opponents became the norm for the U.S. National Team in 1988, a year in which all records for the number of matches played by a U.S. team were broken.

ABOVE / *U.S. fans at the St. Louis Soccer Park cheer their team during a 0–0 duel with El Salvador in a November 1989 qualifying match.* Jon Van Woerden

OPPOSITE / *The U.S. team got a taste of Italy — on and off the field — receiving a noisy introduction to Italy's soccer-crazed fans.* Roberto Koch AC

The goal of making the 1990 World Cup in Italy received new emphasis when on July 4, 1988, FIFA named the United States as the host nation for the 1994 World Cup. Now it would be more than a matter of soccer heritage for the Americans to make it to Italy. Now the whole world would be watching to see how far the game had come in the United States — perhaps using it as a kind of barometer to gauge how successful a World Cup host the Americans might be.

Twenty days following the historic announcement, Osiander's team entered the second round of CONCACAF zone qualifying with two matches against Jamaica. On July 24, in a hot and dusty National Stadium in Kingston, the U.S. squad battled to a 0–0 draw. Three weeks later in St. Louis, the Americans cracked a tense 1–1 match wide open with four second–half goals to win 5–1 and move into the third round of qualifying, which would begin in April 1989.

With the first qualifying hurdle cleared, the Federation's development plan was solidified in October 1988 when 16 American players signed contracts with the Federation to play full time with the U.S. National Team. While somewhat unconventional, the arrangement was necessary not only to avoid conflicting schedule problems for players who otherwise would be playing for other clubs, but also to ensure the continuity of team preparation leading up to the eight remaining qualifying matches in 1989.

The Federation made another move in January 1989 by hiring a full-time U.S. National Team coach, something that hadn't been a part of the U.S. program since 1986. Bob Gansler, at the time the coach of the U.S. Under–20 Team and a veteran Federation staff coach, took the full-time job. Osiander, though stepping aside as the national team coach, continued his Federation coaching by taking an appointment to prepare the U.S. Under–23 Team which would enter qualifying rounds for the 1992 Olympic Games in Barcelona.

Gansler conducted his first training camp for the U.S. team in Irvine, Calif., in late January 1989, followed by a February training session in Florida. With the United States' first of eight World Cup qualifying matches coming up in just two months, Gansler still had some unfinished business with his under–20 squad, which was on its way to the 5th World Youth Championship for the FIFA/Coca–Cola Cup in Saudi Arabia. Major competition for the big team would have to wait a couple of weeks.

Gansler, a resident of Milwaukee, Wisc., who had moved with his family to the United States from West Germany when he was 11, took his U–20's to a history–making fourth place finish in Saudi Arabia, the highest ever finish for an American team in a major FIFA international competition. The Americans nearly made it to the tournament finals, losing to Nigeria — a team that was later sanctioned by FIFA for using overage players — in extra time.

After the Saudi trip, Gansler and his U.S. National Team embarked on a solid 18 months of globetrotting. It began with a trip to South America, from which the team returned with victories

ABOVE / *Tiny Trinidad & Tobago needed only a tie, at home, against the United States to advance to the World Cup tournament. Their fans showed up in red, confident they would soon be "on the road to Italy." What happened? Read on.* Jon Van Woerden

OPPOSITE / *The United States, and defender Michael Windischmann, kicked up its heels for three exhibition matches against flashy, talented Colombia in 1989 and 1990. All three games were played in Miami, and all three resulted in one–goal U.S. losses, still encouraging results against world–class competition.* Jon Van Woerden

over two Paraguayan club teams. That set up the team's debut in front of American crowds at the 1989 Marlboro Cup of Miami at Joe Robbie Stadium, which would provide the final two matches before the team moved into World Cup qualifying matches against Costa Rica. Gansler's team played well, defeating America Cali of Colombia, 2–0, and barely losing to Columbia's Independiente Santa Fe on penalty kicks to place second.

The United States, drawn into a five–team, third–round CONCACAF group (North and Central America, Caribbean nations), traveled to Costa Rica on April 16, 1989, for the first of eight stops on the road to Italia '90. The Americans would have to play the eight matches — home–and–away games against Costa Rica, Trinidad & Tobago, Guatemala and El Salvador — and come out among the top two teams in order to make it to Italy.

The harsh reality of spirited international competition hit the Americans squarely in the face as they marched onto the Estadio Nacional field in front of 26,000 noisy Costa Ricans who had crammed into a facility which held 20,000 comfortably. The vocal enthusiasm shown by the home fans was deafening throughout the match and the celebration continued as the "Ticos" held onto a 1–0 lead to record two points in the qualifying standings. Gansler's team, though disappointed with the loss, then set its sights on the rematch two weeks later in St. Louis.

Before an April 30 sellout crowd at St. Louis Soccer Park and in front of a national televised audience, midfielder Tab Ramos scored a goal and goalkeeper David Vanole blocked a penalty kick in the closing minutes to give the Americans a 1–0 victory and two points.

Two weeks later, on May 13, the U.S. team met Trinidad & Tobago — a team from which it would hear much from before the qualifying round was over — at Murdock Stadium in Torrance, Calif. The United States played well and even dominated for vast stretches of the game, buoyed by a marvelous goal from defender Steve Trittschuh, but in the final minutes, T&T scored a goal to salvage a 1–1 draw and head back to Port of Spain with a point. This would be the match that would come back to haunt the Americans as the qualifying round wound down in November.

The busy schedule of international matches continued two weeks later when Gansler's team competed in the Marlboro Cup of New York, June 2–4, at Giants Stadium in East Rutherford, N.J. The Americans responded with perhaps two of their brighter performances in many years, defeating the heralded Benfica club of Portugal, 2–1, and then blanking the national team of Peru, 3–0, to take the Cup championship. The event also marked the international debut of goalkeeper Tony Meola, who had been invited to the week–long

training camp preceding the two matches. His "training camp" was transformed into a sparkling debut as he entered the nets because of injuries to Vanole and Jeff Duback. It was a role Meola would not relinquish for the remainder of the qualifying run.

Next up was Guatemala, a team which had encountered some difficulty playing well during its initial matches. Gansler, who had predicted that all the U.S. matches would be difficult, with the final outcome not being decided "until they rolled out the final ball in November," knew that Guatemala would again provide all the challenge his young U.S. team could handle.

Forward Bruce Murray got the Americans off to an early start, converting a brilliant crossing pass from midfielder John Harkes by hitting a right–footed full volley directly in front of the net to give the United States a 1–0 lead in the first few minutes. The physical, foul–plagued match, which included one Guatemalan being sent off, was tied in the 22nd minute. It was up to U.S. forward Eric Eichmann to score the winning goal in the 67th minute, giving the Americans two more points.

The Guatemala match ended the United States' summer qualifying schedule and began a three–month gap in the eight–match schedule. During the "break," the Americans took on the best by competing against the national champions of Poland, Ruch Chorzow, Mexico's most popular club, Chivas, Italian club powers Sampdoria, A.S. Roma and Juventus, plus matches against another Italia '90–bound team, South Korea, and the professional champions of the USSR, Dnepr.

The Americans — seeming to relish playing outside the pressure of the World Cup qualifying round — did exceedingly well. The United States won the Marlboro Cup of Chicago, blasting Ruch Chorzow, 3–1, and then surviving a horribly physical test against Chivas to take the win and Cup title on penalties.

Two of the Italian club matches were during a trip to St. Vincent, Italy, and the Baretti Tournament. That European journey would mark the first time the U.S. team would win respect in Italy. Gansler's team played hard, losing 1–0 to Sampdoria, then came back to score three goals in 20 minutes en route to a stunning 4–3 victory over A.S. Roma.

The travel–weary U.S. squad flew straight to Los Angeles for the fourth and final installment of the Marlboro Cup series of 1989, and fell to Juventus, 2–0, and South Korea, 2–1.

Twelve days later — August 25 — a pair of American soccer feats were recorded in a single, wonderful evening of international football at Philadelphia's Franklin Field. An intensely pro–American crowd of more than 43,000 rocked Franklin Field's aging walls as the United States rode Eric Eichmann's goal to a 1–0 victory over Dnepr, the Ukrainian champions of

the Soviet Union's top professional league. The second feat of the evening was the size of the crowd, the largest ever to watch the U.S. National Team play, outside of the 1984 Olympics. Young children and adults alike showed their love for this American team by reaching over barriers to touch the U.S. players as they left the field and besieged the U.S. squad for autographs long after the last shower was taken.

On Sept. 17, the Americans began the home stretch of the qualifying run, this time against El Salvador in a match moved from San Salvador to Tegucigalpa, Honduras, by FIFA because of crowd control problems. Midfielder Hugo Perez, who emigrated to the United States from El Salvador when he was 11, scored the goal that gave the United States a 1–0 victory over his former countrymen. The United States chalked up two more valuable points in the playoff table.

Gansler's team hoped to move closer to clinching a World Cup berth with a win in Guatemala City on Oct. 8. The return match with Guatemala was the sixth playoff game and took place on a field saturated by days of heavy rains. The Americans sloshed through a tough 90 minutes, but were forced to settle for only one point from a 0–0 draw. Guatemala, however, was eliminated.

It was Nov. 5 when the return match was scheduled with El Salvador at St. Louis Soccer Park. The Americans felt they would play better at the smaller St. Louis facility, even though public opinion indicated that the team would draw a sellout crowd at larger facilities. However, the home confines could do little to lift the American team, which played what Gansler would describe as one of its more lackluster matches of the qualifying round, drawing 0–0.

The 0–0 result clinched a 1990 World Cup berth for Costa Rica. The second berth would be decided in the final match of the qualifying series on Nov. 19 when the United States faced Trinidad & Tobago on its home turf. T&T, tied with the United States with nine points in the standings, needed only a tie to reach Italy because of a superior goal differential. For the Americans, there was no choice. They had to win in Port of Spain. The young United States team had landed in a pressure cooker.

What unfolded on the warm, sunny island of Trinidad that November afternoon was a spectacle — for the Trinidad & Tobago people, who boldly anticipated a

victory for their team and a spot in Italia '90 — and a mountainous challenge for the U.S. team. Skeptics — of which there were many in the American media — gave the U.S. team little chance of success in Port of Spain, let alone coming home with the required two points.

Midfielder Paul Caligiuri silenced nonbelievers worldwide and a crowd of 35,000 spectators clad in T&T red by launching a left–footed half volley that dropped into the T&T net and gave the Americans a 1–0 lead in the first half. Caligiuri and his lion–hearted teammates then choked off the T&T attack with tenacious, unrelenting defense and outstanding goalkeeping by Meola to hold on for the victory.

The United States was in the World Cup for the first time since 1950. ■

John Polis

SEA OF RED

Imagine this: The U.S. had to win (not just tie) its final qualifying match, but it was forced to accomplish this at Port of Spain, Trinidad, against a team that had already tied the Americans at Torrance, California . . .

. . . and a team now backed by a rabid, confident crowd of 35,000 people that formed an intimidating "sea of red" in an impressive show of unity they hoped would boost their squad all the way to Italy . . .

. . . but the Americans showed courage in a tight, tense, conservative game, and players such as John Harkes (opposite), Paul Krumpe (right) and Peter Vermes (above) helped earn the United States a trip to the World Cup for the first time in 40 years with a 1–0 victory over Trinidad & Tobago.
Jon Van Woerden

IN THE SPOTLIGHT

The light of the World Cup is blindingly bright, and it is not the warm luminance seen on stage. World Cup light is focused, harsh, unforgiving. Images are exaggerated, not enhanced.

In such a setting, every move of every minute is revealed. Italia '90 was the closest scrutiny ever directed at the U.S. National Team; its players sometimes basked in the glow, at other times they turned away from the glare.

Although there are certainly incidents and events better left in shadow, some of the moments — like treasured photographs — should be taken out of the album, held up to the light and admired.

The U.S. performance against host Italy in Rome, June 14, demands a long look. Never was the glare brighter than on that warm evening in the magnificent Olympic Stadium, with red–white–green Italian flags swirling in a sea of more than 73,000 fans. But the red, white, and blue flew as well — and why not, being Flag Day in the United States — as the U.S. team showed its courage in playing the hosts tight despite losing, 1–0.

"When I walked onto the field, everything was perfect," said midfielder Tab Ramos. "The crowd, the grass, the weather, everything. It's a great stadium for a soccer player. That's a dream, a memory I'll never forget."

Forgetting their opener against Czechoslovakia in Florence was, unfortunately, quite impossible. The first U.S. World Cup match in 40 years — a lifelong dream for each player — turned into a 90–minute nightmare,

a depressing 5–1 beating in which midfielder Eric Wynalda became the first U.S. player to be sent off in the tournament. Although the match generated many dark moments, Paul Caligiuri lit up the history of United States soccer by scoring an outstanding goal, proving to the world that American players possess the ingenuity needed for play at the highest level.

Thirty minutes of play remained. The United States, trailing 3–0, was forming its defensive barrier to repel an attack coming down the right flank.

Caligiuri, well inside his own half of the field, spotted midfielder Lubomír Moravčík about to attempt a risky pass — a chip lobbed laterally into the middle of the field from a distance. He sprinted forward to intercept and, with his first touch, pushed the ball to Bruce Murray without breaking stride.

Murray read his move immediately and tapped the ball right back into Caligiuri's path. Sweeper Jan Kocian angled to cut him off, but committed himself to a slide tackle, which Caligiuri neatly slipped through about 35 yards from the goal. So suddenly had the sequence developed that no other Czechoslovak players were close enough to challenge.

Now only goalie Jan Stejskal was between Caligiuri and the goal. The keeper came out, so Caligiuri pulled the ball with his left foot as he swerved right, then drove a shot along the ground with his right foot. Defender Miroslav Kadlec lunged to stop it, but the ball spun past his leg and into the net.

More than 33,000 fans were in the Nuovo Comunale Stadium that evening, and the U.S. goal was greeted with a tremendous cheer. American flags were scattered throughout the stands, except for two pockets of Czechoslovak fans. Florence has long been a favorite stop for American travelers and students, a fact that the city had demonstrated to the team when it entered the stadium earlier in the day.

Conveyed from their training camp in a luxurious coach, the U.S. team was surrounded by a cheering, chanting mob of fans when the bus drove up to the players' entrance gate. American flags were waved and worn, shouts of "U–S–A" rang out, and the lucky ones with cameras snapped away.

"That was great," said defender John Doyle. "They were just fantastic. At that point, I thought for sure we would play well, and maybe even win."

It didn't turn out that way, of course. Yet four nights later, the U.S. players shook off their depression and fought like tigers against Italy's powerful squad, erasing the black marks scrawled on their reputations by the Czechoslovaks and earning praise from their opponents.

Italy broke through to score after just 11 minutes, setting off a sea of flags fluttering in salute. Anticipating a flood of goals, the crowd buzzed expectantly

ABOVE / *Chris Sullivan moves in for a sliding tackle against Italian captain Giuseppe Bergomi. American players generally agree that playing the Azzurri before a huge crowd at Rome was their biggest thrill, also that their game rose to its best level of the tournament.*
Jon Van Woerden

— yet as the game wore on and the goals didn't flow, the buzz faded into whistles. Squeezed out of the U.S. goalmouth by tenacious marking, Italy eventually retreated and kept its 1–0 lead safe.

Italian captain Giuseppe Bergomi said, "They wouldn't let us play at all, and the fact they were using an extra defender made it difficult for us to find space. They blunted the wings and made it difficult for us to do anything."

Defenders John Doyle and Des Armstrong blanketed Italian strikers Salvatore Schillaci, Gianluca Vialli, and Andrea Carnevale. Schillaci wound up as the tournament's leading scorer with six goals, but the United States was the only team to shut him out. Sweeper and captain Mike Windischmann conducted the team's tempo, slowing play down when necessary. Midfielders Marcelo Balboa, Paul Caligiuri, Jimmy Banks and John Harkes chased and tackled relentlessly, blocking Italy's passing routes.

Much of their success was due to coach Bob Gansler opting for a tighter defensive system than he used against Czechoslovakia. But tactics were only part of the solution. To this framework the players added ferocity.

"Guys came out to practice on Tuesday (two days before the Italy match) and really started banging on each other," said forward Peter Vermes. "Czechoslovakia pushed us around, and we knew if we let the Italians push us around, we'd get buried again."

If hard work begets good fortune, the U.S. team earned a piece of luck with 12 minutes left in the first half. Italy was awarded a penalty, and Vialli faked goalie Tony Meola to the wrong side, but Vialli's hard shot hit the base of the goalpost and bounced away.

"You could see their heads drop a bit, and it pumped our guys up," said Vermes. "After the way things went in the Czechoslovakia game, we were due for a break or two."

Unfortunately, they didn't get break No. 2. Midway through the second half Bruce Murray whipped a free kick around Italy's defensive wall. Goalie Walter Zenga pushed it aside, but Vermes pounced on the rebound and drove it through Zenga's legs from a sharp angle, where it caromed off the goalie's posterior and trickled toward the goal line. Defender Ricardo Ferri, who had committed the foul for which the free kick was given, batted the ball clear before a U.S. player could knock it in.

I still feel I should have stuck it in," said Vermes. "Gosh, it was just hard luck."

Hard times returned for the U.S. team in its final match. Austrian Peter Artner was ejected late in the first half, but the United States failed to take advantage. Austria regrouped at halftime, and burned the American defense twice with lightning–like attacks

ABOVE / *After being intimidated by Czechoslovakia,
American players vowed to
take physical matters in this
rough-and-tumble tourna-
ment into their own hands.
Here John Doyle manhandles
Austria's Manfred Zsak as
both pursue the ball.* Jon Van
Woerden

to take a 2–0 lead. Meola had repeatedly staved off the Austrians in
one–on–one situations, but he had no
chance to stop either goal.

Tab Ramos pulled a slice of magic
out of the hat to set up Murray for a
goal with seven minutes to play.
Ramos slipped a defender on the right
wing by putting the ball between his
legs, then squared a pass to Murray.
Murray's shot hit goalie Klaus Lindenberger on the arm, squirted through
his legs and rolled into the net.

The goal was Murray's ninth international tally, tying him with Ricky
Davis at the top of the U.S. all–time
scoring list. Caligiuri's goal, his
fourth, certainly ranks with his incredible shot against Trinidad & Tobago
as among the most memorable goals
in U.S. history, not far behind Joe
Gaetjens' dramatic winner in the 1950
World Cup upset of England. During
Italia '90 Windischmann extended his
all–time record of international appearances to 53. Murray ended the tournament second on the list with 45 appearances and Caligiuri third with 40.

Yet milestones and marks can't cap-
ture the sensation of stepping into the
World Cup spotlight. Each player took
home the personal prize of participa-
tion as well as collective pride in wear-
ing the U.S. jersey.

"This is our first World Cup, the
first U.S. World Cup in 40 years, and
to play in the World Cup is the greatest moment of my career," said Doyle,
who was a collegiate All–American
and played in the 1988 Olympics.

Meola, first–generation son of Italian immigrants, played in front of relatives from the "old country" as well
as his parents. "I knew it'd be great
to play here, but I wasn't even close,"
he said. "It's heaven for someone like
me, to play in the World Cup in Italy."

"As much as I wanted it for my-
self, I wanted it for my father, too.
When I was a kid, he'd talk to me
about Juventus and the Milan teams,
and the great Italian players. Being
here and being a part of that is
incredible."

Ridge Mahoney

italia '90

UNLIKELY HEROES

The 1990 World Cup started with a shocker: unheralded Cameroon defeated defending champion Argentina, 1-0. What would have been the odds at that point that Argentina would recover sufficiently to reach the final against West Germany?

And who could have foreseen the role penalty shootouts would play in Italia '90? That both semifinal matches between Italy and Argentina and West Germany and England would be decided by soccer's version of Russian Roulette?

What wasn't a surprise was the stellar play of West Germany throughout the tournament. Running on all cylinders, coach Franz Beckenbauer's squad breezed through the qualifying rounds and then held off England in the semifinals and Argentina in the final. The only thing they can be faulted for is not being as overpowering or scoring as much at the end of the Cup as they did at the beginning.

During the tournament, several new faces and stars emerged, although one of the "new" faces was actually an old one — 38-year-old Roger Milla of Cameroon, who captivated the soccer world by scoring four goals while leading Cameroon to the quarterfinals. Then there was the player who captivated the host Italians, their own Salvatore Schillaci, who emerged as a scoring machine.

Those two were among the top players who stood out in a World Cup that would be dominated by defense.

MARADONA, MILLA AND *MILLE GRAZIE*, SCHILLACI

Lothar Matthäus, Germany's midfield conductor, and his shot, timed at 80 miles (130 km)/hour . . .

The bounce in Roger Milla's step, the gap in his grin, his informality with reporters and four great goals all smacked of pure joy unspoiled by the constraints of modern soccer . . .

England's young star, Paul Gascoigne, cried so hard after the semifinal loss to Germany that he walked on to the German bus by mistake . . .

Italy cheered Americans Tony Meola and Paul Caligiuri as one of their own and Salvatore Schillaci became the savior Italy was desperately seeking . . .

And for one inspired moment, Diego Maradona parted Brazil's defense long enough to knock it out of the Cup. Provocative until the end, Maradona's every word and action made headlines . . .

ABOVE / *A young Italian woman beams in pride on the way to another of her heroes' successes, silhouetted against a soft Roman dusk and three of the empire's more historic heroic figures.* Silva / AC

OPPOSITE / *Religion and soccer play dominant roles in Italian lifestyle, though during World Cup month we're not sure in which order they come. Would you care to ask one of these gentlemen his opinion?* Roberto Koch / AC

ITALY: SOCCER SOCIETY

Italians had one thing on their minds: soccer. At one point, the Pope cut short an address so that people could go home and watch *Il Mondiale* on television.

Salvatore "Totò" Schillaci, the newfound hero from Sicily, united Italy and fed its hopes for a fourth World Cup. The serious, intense look on his face lit up like a pinball machine every time he scored.

Schillaci is a Gianni – come – lately. A second – division find, the 26–year–old was unknown outside of Italy before this year. But he was bought by Juventus of Turin, the richest team in Italy, and impressed in his first season.

Schillaci was chosen by the journalists as the best player of Italia '90, but he started the tournament on the bench. From the first time he touched the ball, he scored. After scoring two goals with his head, Schillaci said he would score with his feet against Uruguay. And he did.

THE OPENER:
LIGHTNING STRIKES ARGENTINA

On June 8, the tournament opened with a thunderbolt: Cameroon 1 – Argentina 0.

Cameroon had a disastrous showing in the African Nations Cup in March, and Carlos Bilardo, Argentina's coach, said then his team could score five goals against Cameroon. A team in turmoil, Cameroon also turned in its official list of 22 players late and drew an industrial–sized fine from FIFA. But Cameroon was good and ready for its appointment with Argentina in Milan.

François Omam Biyik's impressive leap and header beat the World Champions. At the moment he headed the ball, his waist was over a foot above his marker Roberto Sensini's head.

Bilardo characterized it the "worst defeat of my life." Argentina had also lost the opener in 1982, but this was a must–win game against a struggling third–world team, which just happened to give a first–class lesson to the world champions. (As a result of FIFA's widely–publicized campaign to punish tactical fouls with red cards and expulsions, Cameroon finished with two men less than Argentina.)

CAMEROON CAME, PLAYED,
AND CONQUERED

After losing to Zambia and Senegal in the African Nations Cup in March, the Indomitable Lions arrived in Italy with their tails between their legs. But, undoubtedly, Cameroon gave us some of the most memorable moments of the World Cup.

Cameroon players scored joyous goals which they celebrated like children. They beat Argentina, Romania, Colombia and took up the mantle of Brazil for playing soccer with grace, joy and skill. Moreover, with four starters disqualified, they gave England — the inventors of the game — a primer in soccer before bowing out.

In 1982, Cameroon was eliminated from the Cup without losing a game. Then, Cameroon and African soccer were the drums in the distance; in 1990, their message came through loud and clear and their point was eloquently made: Africa deserves another representative in the World Cup.

BRAZIL, IS THAT YOU?

Brazil reluctantly accepted coach Sebastião Lazaroni's polemic defensive theories as a cure for recent World Cup failures. For Brazil's festive fans, who somehow always find a way to make it to the Cup, swapping their traditional offensive game and accepting

ABOVE / *The eyes of the world are on captains Lothar Matthäus of West Germany and Diego Maradona of Argentina as they lead their teams onto the field for the final.* Daniel Motz / MOTZSPORTS

Lazaroni's defensive schemes was like swallowing unpleasant medicine. Not really convinced, Brazil's fanatical *torcedores* went along with it anyway. "I don't care if we're no fun to watch," said Lazaroni, "as long as we win."

Brazil's experience in Italy was traumatic. In the end, it lost to Argentina and was left with the bitter taste of the experiment.

Lazaroni was accused of having too many commercial interests, of favoring the European–based players, of playing two attackers instead of three, of playing too defensively. The bottom line is he didn't win. In Brazil, nothing else will do.

REF–RAFF

The refereeing was erratic at best, abysmal at worst. Maradona got away with another hand ball, this time stopping a goal against the Soviets. Swedish referee Erik Fredriksson didn't see it. "The right hand is for scoring goals, the left hand is for stopping them," quipped Brazil's coach.

The referee Edgardo Codesal was also under fire in the final, where his controversial call gave the Germans a penalty.

Joseph Blatter, FIFA's secretary general with a flair for the dramatic, criticized the refereeing and promised reforms. By 1998 all the referees would be professionals, he said. For the problem of too many important matches coming down to penalty kicks — including both semifinals — Blatter was more circumspect: "If somebody's got a better idea, I'd be happy to hear it."

ABOVE / *Nary a frown is to be found on the faces of champions. We also suspect you'd have to travel far to find one right now in West Germany.* David Jacobs / Action Images

GROUP F: FINALLY A RESOLUTION

Group F was another nightmare for FIFA, although the hooligan problem with English and Dutch fans was not as bad as expected. There were disturbances — a few hundred Brits were deported for rousing in Rimini — and there was a stampede in Cagliari.

Ireland's fans were a dream. They stayed 30 minutes waving their flags and singing in appreciation of their team in Rome's Olympic Stadium after losing to the *Azzurri*.

With just two games to go, Group F threatened to finish just as it had started — all even. The final games did untangle things somewhat, but a draw was needed to see if Ireland or the Netherlands would face the powerful West Germans.

The result meant that one of the glamour teams would be knocked out as early as the second round. The Dutch team, torn by intrasquad squabbles and the pressure of being one of the favorites, never put it all together. They played their best against the Germans,

but Jürgen Klinsmann played the "finest game of my career" and the Germans won what was maybe the best game of the Cup.

THE FINAL: THE HOST WAS MISSING

Maradona spiked the punch in Italy's World Cup party by knocking them out of the Cup in an emotionally-charged game in Naples and spoiling the preordained final with West Germany.

As disappointed as Italy was over the outcome, West Germany's victory was deserved. The West Germans had the right mix of skill and power. Their team had matured. Lothar Matthäus, its captain, was a loser in '86. Matthäus controlled midfield, defended, blew past defenders, passed to teammates — and as if that wasn't enough — he also scored goals. And when he raised the Cup to the sky in Rome's Olympic Stadium, it meant that, once again, the Teutons were conquerors in Rome.

Keyvan Antonio Heydari

first round

UPSETS AND UNDERDOGS

Recent World Cups have been stained by stagnant, cautious play in the first round. Fearing defeat, teams are especially careful in their first match, and the two teams obligated to play the tournament's opening match labor under those pressures plus the world's undivided attention.

But the Italia '90 opener on June 8 in Milan offered a most intriguing contrast: titleholder Argentina and 1988 African champion Cameroon. The world champions against the Third World.

Cameroon, bounding and running from the opening kickoff, unsettled Argentina with sheer dynamism — attacking relentlessly, tackling recklessly. Its stunning 1–0 win came at a high price: under tough guidelines dictated by FIFA, referee Michel Vautrot issued three yellow cards and two red to Cameroon players.

So the opener generated two themes for the tournament: tighter refereeing, and beware of the underdogs!

The Indomitable Lions turned to the oldest member of their pride against Romania, June 14, and Roger Milla — elder statesman among field players in the tournament at 38 — dispatched Romania with a pair of goals after coming on as a substitute.

His pair of goals propelled Cameroon into the second round, the first time an African nation had advanced.

Romania advanced as well, despite that loss. Its players had already endured the bloody rebellion that toppled dictator Nicolae Ceaucescu in December, and trouble flared in their country again a few days after they upset the Soviet Union, 2–0, in their tournament opener.

After losing to Cameroon, 2–1, Romania fell behind Argentina, 1–0, in its final group game, but rallied for a 1–1 tie and a spot in the second round. Romania hadn't advanced in four previous appearances. Conversely, the Soviet Union failed to advance for the first time after six consecutive successes.

Czechoslovakia had pulled free from the Communist chokehold more peacefully than Romania, and its players had been trickling to Western Europe for several years. Thousands of Czechoslovak fans took 12–hour bus trips to watch their team in Italy, celebrating dual victories: in soccer and in the formation of the new government with President Václav Havel at its head. The Czechoslovak team and coach Jozef Venglos dedicated their victories to Havel.

As the Communist nation furthest removed from Soviet influence, Yugoslavia had long been exporting its players abroad. This spread the talent around Europe, which complicated preparations for World Cups. Not since 1962 had Yugoslavia made it past the second round, despite stocking the first divisions of Europe with skillful, tricky ballplayers.

This time, though, Yugoslavia kept its focus on Italia '90. Wins over Colombia and the United Arab Emirates assured Yugoslavia of second place in Group D and set the stage for a thrilling second–round match against Spain.

Spain topped Group E by knocking off Belgium, 2–1, in one of the best first–round games. Midfielder Míchel (Miguel González), who had scored all three goals in an earlier 3–1 thumping of South Korea, converted a penalty for his fourth tournament goal.

ABOVE / *Two of Cameroon's Indomitable Lions make a Diego (Maradona) sandwich during their team's shocking victory over Argentina to open World Cup '90. But alas, the defending world champions and their chief miracle worker would still be heard from until the very end of the tournament.* David Jacobs / Action Images

OPPOSITE / *Referees struggled throughout the World Cup to keep a grip on physical play. Sometimes they succeeded, sometimes not. Colombia's Luis Carlos Perea makes his plea for a little less grip over his activities.* David Jacobs / Action Images

The luck of the draw came into play to unscramble Group F. The first four matches ended in ties; going into the last two games, there existed the strong possibility all four teams could finish with equal points and perhaps even identical goal differences.

England solved one problem by beating Egypt, 1–0, to win the group. Egypt drew admiration with a spirited 1–1 tie against the Netherlands, then lost all that goodwill by clogging its penalty area and choking out a 0–0 tie with Ireland.

Playing at the same time as England–Egypt, the Dutch took an early lead over the Irish when Ruud Gullit — playing below his normally spectacular form, yet still better than his inept teammates — broke through to score. Ireland tied the game in the second half, and the two teams —aware of England's impending win — played out the last minutes and took the 1–1 tie. The draw gave Ireland second place and put the Dutch in third.

When Italy was awarded the 1990 World Cup in 1984, Salvatore Schillaci was a 20-year-old striker playing for Messina in Serie B (second division) of the Italian League. Years before, he'd left grade school to help his family cope with the poverty of Palermo.

He turned pro at age 16 and played for Messina until the summer of 1989, when Juventus — impressed by the 23 goals he scored the previous season, which broke Paolo Rossi's Serie B mark — bought him for $6 million. That much for a minor leaguer set off fireworks among the fans and in the press.

After seven months in Serie A, though, the clamor had changed. Now, it was for Italy coach Azeglio Vicini to include Schillaci on the national team. Italy couldn't score goals and Schillaci was banging them in regularly for Juve. Perhaps he could rescue Italy with his deadly finishing, as Rossi had done in leading the *Azzurri* to the 1982 title by scoring six goals.

He was on the substitute's bench when Italy lined up for its opener with Austria on June 9 in Rome. Anxiety born of Italy's goal drought hung over the Olympic Stadium at kickoff, and the nervous twitching and frustration increased as Italy swarmed over Austria yet failed to puncture its shield.

Midway through the second half, a roar rose as Schillaci's short, muscular figure jogged along the sideline. With 16 minutes left to play and the score still 0–0, he ran onto the field as Italian flags waved and shouts of "To-tò Skeel–la–chee" rang out.

Totò is the stage name of one of Italy's funniest comedians. There's nothing humorous in Schillaci's dark features most of the time, but after scoring a goal, his face bursts into pure joy and the dark eyes light up.

Four minutes after entering the match, Schillaci knifed between two Austrian defenders as a cross from Gianluca Vialli sailed into the goalmouth. His header

ABOVE / *West Germany brought its usual powerhouse to the World Cup. With such workmanlike players up and down the roster as Jürgen Klinsmann (No. 18), the Germans marched to the final, with only minor detours like this 1-1 first-round tie with Colombia.* David Jacobs / Action Images

OPPOSITE / *Salvatore Schillaci (No. 19) vaulted from reserve player to Italian national hero in just minutes. His goal against Austria, just four minutes after entering the match, got the Azzurri's moribund offense going and was perhaps the tournament's most dramatic single moment . . .*

(inset) / *. . . while his tally just nine minutes into the contest against Czechoslovakia, punctuated by a celebratory gallop with a teammate, helped his squad to be seeded at the top of Group A. Schillaci led all World Cup scorers with six goals, each one seemingly striking at the moment of maximum dramatic impact.* Daniel Motz / MOTZSPORTS

THE CITY IN THE GOLDEN SHELL

With a city of such rich cultural background, it was fitting that Palermo hosted one of the more diversified and intriguing soccer groups — Group F — in the first round of the World Cup.

Egypt brought with it Arab pride and a reminder that Palermo was occupied by Arabs in the ninth and 10th centuries. England brought the Union Jack and the prospect of a hooligan outbreak, the Netherlands turned the town orange, and Ireland, dear Ireland, brought the smiling faces of appreciative fans.

Perhaps it's also fitting that Group F was considered the toughest bracket of the tournament, what with Palermo, the capital of Sicily, having a reputation for toughness and being linked with the Mafia.

Without question the soccer was fierce — sometimes fiercely boring — with survival (as evidenced by the number of ties — five in six games) seemingly more important than victory. When it was over, England, Ireland and the Netherlands had survived and advanced to the second round, while Egypt, eliminated, garnered respect for its play.

As in many Italian cities, the street markets in Palermo buzz with the aroma of fish, meat herbs and spices and are a constant reminder why Italy is rated by so many as the culinary capital of Europe. However, the local specialty of *stigghioli* — slivers of goat intestines fried in lard — may not appeal to everyone.

Palermo combines the old and the new in an intriguing mix. With the formidable gray mass of Monte Pellegrino at its back and a scenic Italian harbor at its front, Palermo — the city in the Golden Shell (the plain of Conca d'Oro) and once a world capital in the days of the Normans — moves, bristles and fascinates the adventurous. ∎

ABOVE / *Salvatore Schillaci, once roamed the ageless streets of Palermo, as these children now do. But these days Schillaci, or Totò as he is affectionately called by his countrymen, flies over those same roads on national flags proudly emblazoned with his likeness.* Simona Cali Cocuzza / AC

Palermo

ABOVE / *A vendor in Palermo's Mercato del Capo reaches for some of the fruits of the mild Sicilian countryside. The city on Sicily's northern coast hosted three first-round Group F games.*
Roberto Koch / AC

ABOVE / *Did you hear the collective gasp from millions of Argentines as superstar Diego Maradona crumpled to the pitch after a brutal foul at the hands of Cameroon? A full-scale diplomatic summit follows over Maradona's supine body, with the verdict an expulsion meted out against the Lions.* Daniel Motz / MOTZSPORTS

flashed into the net, the Olympic Stadium erupted with joy and relief, and his now–radiant face disappeared in a swarm of blue shirts.

One goal rekindled the hopes of a country and sparked World Cup fever nationwide.

The fervor of Italy's fans helped shroud the fact that teams, with the exception of West Germany, weren't scoring many goals. Led by its terrific trio of Lothar Matthäus, Andreas Brehme and Jürgen Klinsmann — playing on the same field as their club team, Inter Milan — West Germany blasted Yugoslavia in its opener, 4–1, then crushed the hapless United Arab Emirates, 5–1. A 1–1 tie with Colombia slowed the momentum, but still it took Group D and led the scoring with 10 goals.

Brazil and Italy were the only countries to win all three of their first–round games, yet Brazil scarcely impressed anybody. The tougher defensive scheme imposed by coach Sebastião Lazaroni left Brazil's vaunted samba attack barely beating — just four goals in three games, including a 1–0 win over Scotland in which the only goal came after a goalkeeper bobble.

All four South American countries present at Italia '90 reached the second round, but all except Brazil needed luck and nerve to do it. Defending champion Argentina used the "Hand," or more accurately, the "Arm of Maradona" (Defensive Application) to help turn back the Soviet Union, and scraped into the second round by tying Romania, 1–1, and finishing third in Group B.

Daniel Fonseca headed in a free kick with just seconds remaining to lift Uruguay past South Korea, 1–0, and into third place in Group E; Colombia, seemingly knocked out of Group D when West Germany tallied in the 89th minute, struck a stunning equalizer in the last minute when Carlos Valderamma pushed a ball that Freddy Rincón rolled through the legs of goalkeeper Bodo Illgner.

The final totals of 82 goals in 36 matches worked out to a measly average of 2.27 per game. Unfortunately, that average — a product of erratic finishing and cautious play — would persist throughout the competition. Referees handed out 111 yellow cards — a record — and sent off five players, but inconsistency in foul calls and abysmal offside decisions continued to draw the ire of players and fans alike. ∎

Ridge Mahoney

ABOVE (top) / *An all-too-rare sight at World Cup '90: a goal in the making. Brazil's Ricardo Gomes (No. 3) maneuvers toward the Scottish goal . . .*

(middle) / *. . . in the resulting collision and amidst the tangled bodies, the ball scoots away from goalie James Leighton . . .*

(bottom) / *. . . and is tapped into the net by well-placed Müller. This goal, in the 81st minute, was the game's only tally.* David Jacobs / Action Images

GROUP A: SHOWCASE FOR SCHILLACI

As red, green and white Italian flags swirled in the stands and chants of "Eee-tahl-ya!" rang through the refurbished Olympic Stadium in Rome, there also could be felt the peculiar anxiousness unique to soccer: Can we score? And if so, who can score?

Scoring hadn't been a problem for Italy's opponent, Austria. The Austrians had rattled in 10 goals during their five warm-up games, and striker Toni Polster rang up 33 during his club season with Sevilla of Spain.

Yet with the first kick of the Group A opener on June 9, Italy took control. Its defense was typically airtight. Italy swept down the flanks and through the middle, pouring shots in on Klaus Lindenberger in the Austrian goal.

But the famine — only one goal in its last five matches — persisted. Strikers Gianluca Vialli and Andrea Carnevale couldn't convert Italy's superiority into goals. Lindenberger snuffed Carnevale when he broke through, thwarted a deflected shot from Luigi De Agostini, and beat back a vicious drive from Roberto Donadoni. Carnevale misfired in the 34th minute, scooping a cross from Paolo Maldini over the bar from just six yards out.

Fate mocked the Italians as well. Carlo Ancelotti hit the goalpost with a long-range shot, and Brazilian referee José Roberto Wright waved off appeals for a penalty in the 63rd minute when defender Kurt Russ missed a tackle and tripped Donadoni on the left side of the penalty area.

Ten minutes later, with the match grinding toward a 0-0 tie, Italian coach Azeglio Vicini removed Carnevale and brought on Juventus striker Salvatore Schillaci for only his third international appearance.

Schillaci took just four minutes to seduce a nation. Vialli got free near the right wing corner flag and crossed the ball into the goalmouth to Schillaci, lurking between two defenders. Schillaci stabbed the ball past Lindenberger with a fierce header, setting off a tremendous roar of celebration and relief as he ran into the arms of his teammates. All of Rome, all of Italy celebrated as well.

One night later, the United States took on Czechoslovakia in Florence. Its first World Cup appearance in 40 years turned into disaster, as the U.S. team ran into a Czechoslovak buzzsaw and was taken apart, 5-1.

After cautiously sizing up the United States, Czechoslovakia took the lead in the 26th minute. Luboš Kubík stripped Tab Ramos of the ball. In swept teammate Tomas Skuhravý who worked a one-two with Ivo Knoflíček that gave Skuhravý an easy shot past goalie Tony Meola.

Five minutes before the end of the first half, Czechoslovakia scored again after sweeper and captain Mike

FORTY YEARS OF FRUSTRATION ENDS

A merican soccer players get used to laboring in relative obscurity for far less money than most of their foreign counterparts and other pro athletes in their own nation. Perhaps for this reason they sound evangelical when discussing their devotion to the sport, and the responsibility they carried into Italia '90 as the first U.S. World Cup team since 1950.

For many of the players, they are reviving the immigrant heritages of their families by their soccer success. Goalie Tony Meola's father Vinnie played a year of reserve ball with the Avellino club before emigrating to America. Tab Ramos' father played in Uruguay. John Harkes' dad scrapped in the amateur divisions of Scotland, and Bruce Murray's father played professional ball for Scottish clubs.

Marcelo Balboa, son of an Argentinean pro player, got his first taste of World Cup fever by watching Argentina host and win the 1978 tournament. John Stollmeyer's father learned his soccer in Trinidad & Tobago and played at Penn State. Peter Vermes' dad gave up his pro career with Hungarian club Honved Budapest when Soviet tanks rolled into the country in 1956.

Yet for every U.S. World Cup player raised on a European or South American diet of soccer, there's one from the middle-class suburbs where youth soccer has mushroomed in the past decade. Eric Wynalda, Paul Krumpe, David Vanole and Paul Caligiuri hail from Southern California, an area that produces many of the country's top collegiate players and birthplace of the American Youth Soccer Organization. Northern California yielded John Doyle. Jimmy Banks grew up in Milwaukee's inner city and Desmond Armstrong took up soccer when his family moved from Washington, D.C. to the Maryland suburbs.

Call them America's team. ■

Ridge Mahoney

RIGHT / *Its first World Cup match in 40 years was one the United States would rather erase from memory — a 5-1 drubbing at the hands of Czechoslovakia. Here Tab Ramos tries to control the ball in front of the Czech net with the help of defender Desmond Armstrong (No. 15). No goal resulted.* Daniel Motz / MOTZSPORTS

Windischmann intercepted a loose ball but let Ivan Hašek pick it off his foot. Windischmann brought him down in the box and Michal Bílek gave Meola no chance by cracking his penalty kick into the top corner.

Reeling from this one–two punch, the United States got belted again five minutes into the second half when Hašek headed in a corner kick from Jozef Chovanec. Things hit bottom for the United States less than three minutes after falling behind, 3–0. Eric Wynalda was baited into shoving Lubomír Moravčík, and referee Kurt Roethlisberger curiously showed Wynalda the red card. It was the first time a U.S. player had been ejected from a World Cup tournament match.

Paul Caligiuri temporarily gave the United States some relief in the 60th minute by scoring one of the best goals of the tournament with a superb piece of skill. He intercepted a square pass in midfield and pushed a ball that Bruce Murray played right back as Caligiuri ran into the Czechoslovak half. Sweeper Jan Kocian tracked back and had every chance to stop him, but Caligiuri neatly slipped through his slide tackle before cutting around goalkeeper Jan Stejskal and slotting the ball along the ground from a sharp angle.

The U.S. flurry ebbed, though, once Czechoslovakia recovered from Caligiuri's stunner. Skuhravý sealed the victory by powering through defender Steve Trittschuh to head home another corner kick in the 79th minute. Substitute Milan Luhový knocked in a fifth goal in the final seconds.

Four days of criticism of the United States in the world press followed. The Roman Colosseum was suggested as a more appropriate venue than the Olympic Stadium, since the match-up with Italy would certainly be a modern version of Lions vs Christians. Yet on June 14, Italy thankfully accepted another 1–0 victory it found much tougher than the impressive showing against Austria.

The United States presented a cautious, disciplined front to the host Ital-

ABOVE / *Wynalda's expulsion brought him to scratch his head in amazement and wonder. He wasn't alone. The international press thought the call hasty and bizarre at best, downright wrong at worst. Nonetheless, Wynalda will be the answer to the trivia question, "Who was the first U.S. player to be red-carded from a World Cup match?"* Steve Hale / Action Images

OPPOSITE / *Frustration is painted all over Eric Wynalda's face as the U.S. forward struggles to tackle Czechoslovakia's Michal Bílek. Wynalda was later ejected from the game.* David Jacobs / Action Images

ians, playing the ball laterally and back to Meola for much of the game even though it fell behind, 1–0, in the 11th minute. A crowd roaring in expectation of a rout quieted in the second half as Italy's attacks broke down against a tenacious U.S. defense, and their frustration rained down on their team at the final whistle. Fans began streaming up the steps with 15 minutes left, an extraordinary breach of protocol for the host team.

U.S. coach Bob Gansler sat down three players who started against Czechoslovakia, bringing Jimmy Banks and Marcelo Balboa into midfield and John Doyle into the defense.

Those adjustments, plus a much more rigid scheme, took the game away from Italy, even though Giuseppe Giannini scored after just 11 minutes.

If not for a double save by Italian goalie Walter Zenga midway through the second half, the United States might have pulled off a far more sensational feat: tying Italy. Bruce Murray bent a free kick that Zenga had to knock away, and Peter Vermes streaked in from the left to shoot the rebound. It got under Zenga's outstretched leg but struck his rump and dribbled toward the goal line, where Riccardo Ferri booted it to safety. Italy had been literally saved by the backbone of its sturdy defense.

One night later, the Czechoslovaks lined up against Austria aiming for their first second–round appearance since they reached the 1962 final. Two points would do it, and in a bitter, foul–marred match in Florence, they carved out a 1–0 win on Bílek's penalty. Czechoslovak flags — the other nation of red, white and blue ensconced in this ancient city — danced in the stands and through the streets.

Austria, whose mood grew darker as the tournament progressed, gave away the penalty after 30 minutes of play. Defender Anton Pfeffer tapped a back pass that Chovanec darted in to steal as Lindenberger charged out. The goalie's desperate dive caught Chovanec instead of the ball; Chovanec suffered a pulled thigh muscle on the foul, and was flat on his back near the signage boards as Bílek slid his shot past Lindenberger. Then he ran over to the prone Chovanec and slid into an embrace.

So, when Group A concluded on June 19, first place was up for grabs between Czechoslovakia and Italy in Rome, while Austria and the United States battled for the spoils.

Schillaci sent Italy on its way with a 2–0 win by heading in a misfired volley from Giannini in the ninth minute. His new forward partner, Roberto Baggio, electrified the Olympic Stadium by accepting a pass in midfield and slaloming through the Czechoslovak defense to score a brilliant goal in the 77th minute. The victory assured Italy of the group title and the right to

TIPTOE IN, TIPTOE OUT

T he Swedish team tiptoed in and out of Italy with hardly anybody noticing. It gave a lesson in anonymity. Losing all three of their first–round games put the Swedes on a par with the United States and the Emirates — a disastrous turn-about for a team that had finished ahead of semi-finalist England in the European qualifying phase and which had not lost a match in a tough group.

Because of its qualifying performance, coach Olle Nordin's team was considered among the dark horses for Italy, and before leaving Stockholm, Nordin had oozed confidence. "The program suits us fine," he said.

There are few logical excuses for three dismal 2–1 defeats in Sweden's return to the World Cup after a 12–year absence. All three games were scheduled for 9 p.m. in northern cities where the heat was unlikely to upset Scandinavian bio–rhythms. Nordin was able to field a basically stable team, though captain Glenn Hysen was unavailable for the opening match against Brazil and looked off–key in the center of the defense when he returned.

Much–vaunted forwards Mats Magnusson and Johnny Ekström were so far below par that it was left to the 20–year–old forward Tomas Brolin to sweep up the scraps of praise directed at Nordin's team. Brolin, who played no part in the qualifying phase, was the only bright note.

"There are no excuses," said a saddened Nordin after Sweden had thrown away a 1–0 lead and lost, 2–1, to Costa Rica. "The simple truth is that we came to this World Cup with high hopes, but for some rea-son we never managed to get our game together." ■

Graham Turner

LEFT / *Sweden's Klas Ingesson (No. 10) attempts to drive around David McPherson of Scotland. Most experts predicted the solid Swedes would advance to the second round, but they joined the list of teams that disappointed and took an early trip home by losing consecutive 2-1 decisions to Brazil, Scotland and Costa Rica.*
Daniel Motz / MOTZSPORTS

ABOVE / *There's typically no subtlety among international soccer fans, nothing left to chance or guess as to allegiance. These fans are from — let's see, now — Colombia . . .* David Jacobs / Action Images

RIGHT / *. . . and these boosters come from — that's right, you're getting the hang of it — Italia. The lion likes the* Azzurri, *too, but he's spitting mad at being climbed on all the time by celebrating soccer fans . . .* Roberto Koch / AC

LEFT / *. . . While more understated in game attire and conduct, these gentleman are obviously interested in the progress of the United Arab Emirates. In fact, the man in white is Emir Hamdin bin Zayed Al Nahyan, president of his country's soccer federation and son of the UAE's ruling emir, Abu Dabni . . .* Marco Bruzzo / AC

TARTAN (RE)TREAT

S cotland surprised nobody by being eliminated in the first round for the seventh time in seven World Cups. At least the Scots managed a win against Sweden. In six previous competitions they had beaten only Zaire, the Netherlands and New Zealand.

The loss of Richard Gough after just 45 minutes of the tournament was a major blow to the defense. Some key players were merely blurred images. And coach Andy Roxburgh was an academic with no experience at club level.

Roxburgh couldn't invoke the surprise factor as the reason for the disastrous opening defeat to Costa Rica. After watching Costa Rica beat the United States in Miami four months earlier, he had confessed to being "unpleasantly surprised by the standard of their play." He was also unpleasantly surprised by a lackluster midfield, which at times was so apathetic that the 20,000-strong Tartan Army — which gave the team otherwise immaculate support — made its displeasure known.

Roxburgh also faces questioning about the constant shuffling of his squad. Seven players participated in all three games, yet 11 more were used to fill the remaining four berths. He failed to find an attacking pair. The Scots scored twice in 270 minutes, and only South Korea and Egypt scored fewer goals. In Scotland's one stirring performance against Sweden, Roxburgh incorporated a third forward into the formation and adopted an aggressive approach. In the final game against Brazil, though, Scotland reverted to its conservative ways and was eliminated. ■

Graham Turner

RIGHT / *Scotland's Alex McLeish applies flying defense to a thrust from Brazilian Alemão (No. 5). That pretty much typified the Scots' tourney — tough on defense, but not enough offense. They scored in just one of three games.* David Jacobs / Action Images

defenders plus two defense–minded midfielders and invited Sweden to provide the attacking soccer.

For half an hour Brazil was unrecognizable in a match tough enough to warrant yellow cards for José Mozer, Dunga (Carlos Verri) and Branco (Claudio Leal), plus one for Sweden's Joakim Nilsson. The Swedes tried valiantly to break down the massed ranks of the Brazilian defense, and discovered in the speedy 20–year–old Tomas Brolin a forward of great promise. Brazil scored in the 39th minute on a masterful pass from left–back Branco into the path of Careca (Antonio Oliveira) who rounded Swedish goalie Thomas Ravelli, tucked the ball in the net and veered off to dedicate a lambada to the fans.

Seventeen minutes into the second half he struck again. This time Müller (Luiz Costa), the striker controversially preferred to megastars Bebeto (José Oliveira) and Romàrio Faria, reached the endline on the right and squared the ball for Careca to score with ease. Sweden scored with 12 minutes remaining when Brolin took a pass from Jonas Thern past Mozer to beat goalie Claudio Taffarel. Brazil held on for a morale–boosting win.

Lazaroni's workmanlike team was confident of further morale boosters when it opened the second round of games against Costa Rica six days later. The match had been billed as 130 million Brazilians against 2–1/2 million Costa Ricans; David against Goliath; and even the hare against the tortoise. The hare won, but with a helping push from the tortoise when Costa Rican stopper Montero helped a Müller shot past his own goalie in the 33rd minute to notch the only score of a 90–minute non–event. Brazil had 23 shots and took 13 corners. Costa Rica tallied zero and zero.

Brazil's flimsy result fueled criticism from former stars such as Pelé, Socrates and Falcão against a conservative playing system that failed to translate dominance into goals.

Later that evening, the Scots kept their hopes alive with a 2–1 win over Sweden.

Scotland's Roxburgh made four changes for that game and coach Olle Nordin made two in this battle between European teams which had been disappointments in their opening games. Sweden failed to make its superior skill the deciding factor against the fast, furious and gutsy Scots. Scotland drew blood after 10 minutes when David McPherson got the ball to McCall to score at the far post.

Roxburgh had planned the game with a more adventurous 4–3–3 alignment, but when the Scots began to run out of steam in the second half, he replaced winger Gordon Durie with midfielder Paul McStay and put the brakes on to protect the lead. Yet Scotland went further ahead in the 81st minute when Roy Aitken was bundled over by Roland Nilsson, and Johnston con-

ABOVE (left) / *Two Colombians provide an armed escort for Yugoslavia's Dragan Stojković as he dashes wildly up the pitch . . .*

(right) / *. . . until, at last, Stojković surrenders and heads the ball away. His team did not surrender, however — Yugoslavia won the first-round encounter, 1–0.*
David Jacobs / Action Images

verted the penalty. Scotland's joy lasted five minutes. Then substitute Glenn Strömberg volleyed home a cross from Anders Limpar and the Scots hung like grim death for the final four minutes.

The result left both European teams with their backs to the wall in the third round of matches. Sweden needed a handsome win over Costa Rica, which needed a point, while Scotland needed a point against the Brazilians, who had already qualified.

This inspired Lazaroni to contemplate nine changes in order to rest his stars. But a delegation of players headed by Careca struck a blow for player power by storming in and blocking all but two of the changes — Ricardo Rocha for the suspended Mozer, and Romàrio for Müller. Roxburgh reverted to a cautious 4–4–2 in search of a draw and came within nine minutes of obtaining it.

As a substitute, Müller scored the goal that gave Brazil the victory. The 1–0 score meant another miserly, uncharacteristic result for the prosaic Brazilians and another early trip home for the Scots, who have now hit the self–destruct button in the first phase of the last five World Cups.

Costa Rican goalkeeper Luis Gabelo Conejo prefaced the game against Sweden with his usual prayer session and ended it convinced that they had been answered. For a full hour the desperate Swedes monopolized the ball, the play, the chances and the ambitions, but their over–haste resulted in pumping high balls towards Conejo. Sweden's 32nd minute goal came from a set play.

After an hour, Costa Rica coach Bora Milutinovic decided to replace midfielder Roger Goméz (one of four players booked) and send on Hernán Medford, a winger he claimed was too fast to last more than half an hour. The impact was immediate. The Swedish defenders needed long lenses to focus on the fast–disappearing red blur, and in the 75th minute Stefan Schwarz earned himself a yellow card for a grid–iron tackle on the right. Cayasso floated in the free kick, and there was skipper Flores to head it past Ravelli. Three minutes from time, Medford sprinted clear yet again to score the second goal. The Swedes and Scots limped away from Group C to lick their wounds. Brazil gained a passing mark, nothing more. But it was fiesta time back in San José. ∎

Graham Turner

It came as little surprise that West Germany won Group D with seemingly a minimum of effort while scoring 10 goals in three games.

From the moment Lothar Matthäus put the Germans ahead in the 28th minute against highly–rated Yugoslavia, it was obvious that Franz Beckenbauer's team would live up to its pre–tournament expectations.

West Germany went on to defeat Yugoslavia, 4–1, a result that became even more credible given its opponent's later success in the competition.

The strength of Germany is not just in who's on the field, but who isn't as well. On the bench were Karlheinz Riedle, who had just joined Lazio from Werder Bremen for $8 million; Andreas Möller, rated in the same price bracket; and the reliable Pierre Littbarski.

Beckenbauer, who had announced his pending retirement after Italia '90 earlier in the season, had one more ambition as coach: to become the first person to captain and coach his country to World Cup titles. His team had started perfectly.

In 1974 Beckenbauer, a stylish sweeper, led the Germans to the World Cup championship over the Netherlands in Munich before embarking on a career with the New York Cosmos.

That German team of the early seventies is reckoned to be the best ever by its supporters, so when Beckenbauer compared his 1990 squad with such illustrious predecessors it was praise indeed.

Yugoslavia was to show that it was a skillful, intelligent team but against the rampant Germans it was very much second best.

Matthäus, who plays in Milan for Internazionale, scored twice against Yugoslavia, one a magnificent individual effort. Germany had given notice to the rest of the world what it could expect.

Like Beckenbauer, Matthäus is an inspiration. Such is his versatility he could fill any outfield position to a level a specialist player would be proud of.

The way he drives his team from midfield with surging runs into the opponent's penalty area has become the hallmark of the German team and never was it better illustrated than in the captain's performance against Yugoslavia.

In its next match, Germany scored five goals against the United Arab Emirates, which was making its first appearance in the World Cup. The surprise was that the UAE scored once and the name of Khalid Ismail Mubarak goes in the history books as the scorer of his country's first goal at this level.

The Germans didn't get out of third gear — they didn't need to — although the UAE offered some stubborn resistance before it bowed out.

ABOVE / *West Germany squared off against Colombia in one of the more entertaining matches of the first round. Here Pierre Littbarski (No. 7), who scored the German goal, battles with Colombia's Gildardo Gómez.*
David Jacobs / Action Images

The UAE returned home with the worst record of all the competitors — three defeats, two goals scored and a total of 11 conceded, after the final 4–1 defeat by Yugoslavia.

But simply to score two goals was something of an achievement for the Emirates, which had dismissed Mario Zagalo, the Brazilian coach two months after they had qualified for Italy.

Zagalo's successor was a Pole, Bernard Blaut, who took the UAE to the 10th Gulf Cup earlier in 1990, where it failed to win a game, losing even to tiny Bahrain.

ENERGETIC EFFORT

C ontrary to popular belief, the U.S. National Team wasn't the only country to qualify despite lacking a domestic pro league. This tiny Arab nation of 1.6 million — by far the smallest population among the 24 contestants — reached the World Cup for the first time despite fielding a team of amateurs. The players do, however, receive bonuses and gifts for their soccer exploits.

Striker Khalid Ismail Mubarak is a good example. He works at the Dubai airport and plays for Al–Nasr. He debuted with the national team in 1985, and struck a blow for his nation by scoring a goal against West Germany in UAE's second World Cup match. UAE lost, 5–1, yet Mubarak's goal earned him the promise of a Rolls Royce from a businessman, and his energetic play brought contract feelers from clubs in Greece and France.

In fact, each player on the team received more than $250,000 just for qualifying. Oil money runs deep for heroes of sport, amateurs or not.

The UAE lost all three of its matches, scoring two goals and allowing 11, yet drew applause for its effort despite being badly outmanned. Perhaps its Brazilian influence will continue, for coach Carlos Alberto Parreira was offered a one–year extension of his contract following the tournament.

His task will not be easy. There are only about 200 players in the entire country. However, there are signs of progress — the soccer federation is considering the formation of a pro league and the return of foreign players, who were banned in 1982. ■

Ridge Mahoney

RIGHT / *United Arab Emirates shocked the soccer world when it qualified for the World Cup for the first time. Once in Italy, though, reality hit, and the UAE was outscored 11-2 in its three matches, including this 2-0 loss to Carlos Valderrama and* **Colombia.** David Jacobs / Action Images

The Emirates finished at the bottom of the Gulf Cup for the first time in its 20–year history, resulting in the dismissal of Blaut.

The UAE went back to Carlos Alberto Parreira, one of its former coaches who had taken Kuwait to the 1982 World Cup. The Brazilian knew the UAE's style and its players.

He must also have known what he was up against when 12 squad members failed to turn up for a flight to France where the Emirates were training. The remainder, strict Moslems, had stayed on for the Eid al–Fitr feast to mark the end of Ramadan.

Money is no object in the oil–rich Emirates, where the man who picks up the tab is 25–year–old Emir Hamdan bin Zayed Al Nahyan, president of the football association and son of the UAE's ruler.

Just reaching Italy for its first–ever World Cup was a magnificent achievement and now the Emirates must use its success as a base and build on.

Colombia arrived at the World Cup with a reputation for open, attacking football. While the South Americans ultimately were a disappointment, they left behind some positive memories, notably from their midfield inspiration Carlos Valderrama.

ABOVE / *An attack into the heart of Colombian territory by West German Lothar Matthäus (No. 10 White) has set off sirens among those assigned to defend Colombia's goal. This foray was repulsed.*
David Jacobs / Action Images

The South Americans began with a regulation 2–0 win over the UAE, which was no more than was expected of Colombia.

They were then beaten, 1–0, by Yugoslavia, courtesy of a superbly struck goal by defender Davor Jozić, his second of the tournament.

Inevitably it was René Higuita, the goalkeeper who cannot forget he started his career as a striker, who caught the eye.

They call him El Loco (the madman), the sweeperkeeper, because Higuita thinks nothing of charging out of his penalty area to make a tackle a defender would be proud of.

He saved a penalty against Yugoslavia with almost nonchalant ease and then, typically, dribbled the ball away. Most goalkeepers would have theatrically held onto the ball, accepted the backslaps from teammates and then restarted play.

Not Higuita, who never does the predictable. In fact, the only thing that is predictable about El Loco is that he will always surprise you.

In its final game against West Germany, Colombia played its best football to draw 1–1 and therefore qualify for the next phase.

Colombia was wasteful in front of the goal as surprising gaps were found in the German defense.

When Colombia failed to take advantage of a number of scoring opportunities and Littbarski gave Germany a lead in the 88th minute, it seemed as if the South Americans would be on the next plane to Bogotá.

But Freddy Rincón's goal, scored in injury time, was the cue for scenes of uncontrollable joy on the Colombian bench. The Germans have become the master of late goals over the years but, on this occasion, the Colombians upstaged their opponents.

If there was a sour note to the Colombians' success it was their exaggeration of pain.

The most innocuous tackle seemed to bring about an expression of excruciating pain, yet a minute or so later the Colombians would be running around with no after effects.

Yugoslavia duly beat the UAE, 4–1, in its last first–round game to clinch second place in the group behind the Germans, but little had been seen of Dragan Stojković, who was to join Olympique Marseille from Red Star Belgrade in an $8 million deal.

Stojković's departure to French football was merely another example of how Yugoslavia has become the greatest exporter of talent in Europe.

The country has not been subject to the ''export'' restrictions — though recently lifted — of some Eastern European countries. France, particularly, has benefited by signing top-class players at bargain counter prices, although these fees are now set at a more realistic market level.

Yugoslavia was a semifinalist in the inaugural World Cup in 1930 but had reached that stage only once subsequently, in 1962.

Too often it failed to do itself justice at the highest level, despite a number of gifted individuals. Yugoslavia has a tendency to collapse when things start to go against it.

In the first round Yugoslavia showed both sides of its character, having played both badly and well.

Ultimately, Group D finished as most experts had predicted — West Germany, Yugoslavia, Colombia, UAE.

It was one of the few occasions in Italia '90 when the form book proved a reliable guide. ■

Christopher Davies

ABOVE / *Gildardo Gómez and his fellow Colombian defenders had their hands full with such potent German offensive threats as Jürgen Klinsmann. The Colombians performed well in the 1–1 tie with the eventual champions.* David Jacobs / Action Images

RIGHT / *Carlos Valderrama of Colombia is an interesting visual study, even when in repose.* Steve Hale / Action Images

LEFT (top) / *OK now, let's see if we can get this straight: Lothar Matthäus sends Gabriel Gómez flying . . .*

(bottom) / *. . . Matthäus and Carlos Valderrama flatten each other . . .*

RIGHT (top and bottom) / *. . . and Matthäus trips up Leonel Alvarez . . .*

. . . all in the course of one afternoon. We have more, but you get the picture. West Germany and Colombia went at each other fearlessly for most of the match, then suddenly decided to turn their attention to the nets, scoring two goals in the final two minutes — one apiece. David Jacobs / Action Images

OPPOSITE / *For most teams, Carlos Valderrama (the lionlike) would be more than enough color. But Colombia is also blessed with goalie René Higuita, also known as "El Loco" or "the crazy" for his daring, flamboyant style of play in goal. Together he and Valderrama form the "Hairdo Duo."* David Jacobs / Action Images

HERMIT KINGDOM BOWS OUT QUIETLY

S outh Korea's record during the eighties, which included a berth in the 1986 World Cup, proves that it was a force in Asia during that decade.

To leave Italia '90 with no points and just one goal, albeit from a demanding group, was a disappointment. The Koreans clearly paid for not playing against more European countries as part of their preparation.

Korea met only Norway and Malta in preparation games, and, by doing so, missed out on playing against the type of opposition awaiting them in Italy.

The Koreans played well at times but stamina was a problem and too often they were tactically naive. Korea was impressive running at opponents and building up attacking movements but was exposed when it lost possession. It forgot to keep men back and paid the price.

There were consolations. Its goal, a perfectly struck shot from 22 yards by Hwang Bo–kwan against Spain, was one of the best of the tournament.

Several players did well — goalkeeper Choi In–young was invariably busy and did more than was expected of him; defender Chung Jong–soo was steady.

Kim Joo–sung, the pin–up boy of Korean football, he of the flowing locks, did little to show why he was rated Asia's best player. The speed and finishing power Kim showed in the qualifying games deserted him in Italy.

Korea was unfortunate not to draw with Uruguay, which won thanks to an injury–time header from Daniel Fonseca.

Only for a spell against Spain did the Koreans seriously threaten to win a match.

Christopher Davies

LEFT / *South Korea's Park Kyung–joon is fenced in by Belgians, a feeling that must have become familiar to him and to his teammates. The Koreans, relative newcomers to the World Cup, scored just one goal in three matches and joined the United States, United Arab Emirates and Sweden as the only squads to lose all three of their first–round matches.* David Jacobs / Action Images

"Belgium is an excellent, solid unit which doesn't make mistakes," said Tabárez afterwards. "We also have excellent players, but we make mistakes."

Four days later in Udine, Tabárez and his men flirted with sudden death for 91 minutes against a South Korean team condemned to play the last 20 minutes with 10 men after the red card was harshly shown to Yoon Deuk-yeo for time-wasting. In a match punctuated by a first-round record of 58 fouls (South Korea also set a record with 88 fouls in three games, 17 of them to Kim Joo-sung), Uruguay's error was failing to capitalize on its chances. The first-round statistics reveal that Uruguay had more shots at goal (43) than any other Group E team, but scored only two goals.

Skipper Francescoli set the pattern by hitting the post in the first minute. Then Sosa, alone before Choi In-young, shot straight at him. Carlos Aguilera, who had replaced the convalescent Santiago Ostolaza after the break, rattled the woodwork again within a minute. And Choi In-young thwarted the increasingly disjointed and panic-stricken Uruguayans with a string of fine saves.

Their late, late face-saver was so late that the Belgians and Spaniards had finished the other simultaneous match and were in the shower when a long cross from the right found substitute Daniel Fonseca, on for the demoralized Sosa after 72 minutes, completely unmarked and able to place his header into the far corner of the net. Tabárez and his men then retired to celebrate their miraculous survival.

Spain and Belgium, already qualified, were playing only for their group placings in Verona. After a couple of days relaxing by the pool at the Villa Quaranta in Pescantina, the Belgians played with a half-hearted foot on the gas while the Spaniards, able at last to play free from tension, expressed themselves fluently in a creditable 2–1 win. Coach Luis Suárez had reshuffled the defense to play a sweeper (Genaro Andrinúa), two toppers (Manuel Sanchís and Real Sociedad's Alberto Górriz, making his World Cup debut at 32) with Chendo (Miguel Porlan) and Villaroya covering the flanks. Up front, the lanky Julio Salinas replaced Manolo as partner to Butragueño.

In an enjoyable, flowing game, the goals came in a 12-minute first-half spurt. Míchel hit his fourth of the tournament thanks to a 26th minute penalty by Preud'homme on Salinas. Belgium's Patrick Vervoort equalized four minutes later with a deflected free kick. And Górriz rounded off a hat-trick of set-play goals by heading in a 39th minute corner. Scifo, generally well controlled by Roberto (Roberto Fernández Bonillo), should have tied the match from the penalty spot on the hour, but the Belgian schemer imitated Sosa and lifted his shot against Andoni Zubizarreta's crossbar.

ABOVE (top) / *Rubén Sosa of Uruguay takes an unplanned trip to the turf . . .*

(bottom) / *. . . and Spain's Roberto can't understand why.*
David Jacobs / Action Images

The results left Spain topping the group and improving ominously, with Belgium looking serious and solid. Uruguay survived by the skin of its teeth. And South Korea traveled home without a point and with its coach, Lee Hoe-taik, handing in his resignation.

Graham Turner

When the draw was made Group F was nicknamed the Group of Death. With European champions the Netherlands and England, rapidly improving Republic of Ireland and emerging Egypt meeting each other, it was generally considered the most difficult group of all.

By the end of the first round it was known as the Group of Slumber; none of the six games had really captured the imagination of the rest of the world.

The England–Ireland match, which ended 1–1, prompted one Italian newspaper to write the headline: "No Football Please, We're British."

The Netherlands was clearly below the standard it set for itself when it won the 1988 European Championships in such flamboyant style, while Egypt's packed defense and time-wasting tactics did not make for spectacular soccer.

England won the group by virtue of beating Egypt by a solitary header from Mark Wright.

The success was a relief for England's coach Bobby Robson, whose life on and off the field had dominated the sports and news pages in the English tabloids and who was leaving the team after the World Cup.

The controversy surrounding Robson was a cloud over the English squad as it flew to Italy. Inevitably, with almost as many news reporters as sports journalists following England (nominally to report on any trouble English supporters may cause), there were more off-the-field stories.

It was in this atmosphere that England played its opening three games. It had been beaten, 1–0, by Ireland in the 1988 European Championships, but was confident of revenge against a team that had lost only twice in three years.

When Gary Lineker, top scorer in the 1986 World Cup, gave England an early lead it seemed that victory was at hand, but once again Ireland showed

ABOVE / *Taher Abou Zeid of Egypt and Ireland's Paul McGrath handsomely choreograph their movement as they gracefully ascend, but they forget one little detail — the ball.* David Jacobs / Action Images

the qualities that had made it one of the most difficult teams in the world to beat.

Ireland is not pretty to watch but it is pretty difficult to beat. The Irish prefer route–one soccer — playing the ball over the midfield to their strikers, which football purists scorn.

Whatever outsiders think of it, no one in Ireland was complaining. It had brought the Irish unprecedented success, and when Kevin Sheedy tied the score in the second half, it was further proof that coach Jack Charlton's system was, if nothing else, effective.

If that game was awful as a spectacle, Egypt's 1–1 draw with the Netherlands was further proof of the improvement in African football.

Even though Wim Kieft gave the Dutch the lead, Egypt continued to do the simple things well, defending intelligently and causing problems on the counterattack.

It was from one such move that Egypt scored late in the game. The Netherlands' Erwin Koeman felled Ibrahim Hassan in the penalty area and Magdyi Abed El Ghani converted from that spot.

England was unfortunate not to defeat the Dutch. England thought it had won when Stuart Pearce's free kick beat Hans van Breukelen, but to the relief of the Dutch it was an indirect free kick and the ball touched no one as it sped to the back of the net.

It was an encouraging performance by England, which had used a sweeper (*libero*) system, a rare break from its traditional four–man defensive formation. While England was improving it was obvious the Netherlands still had problems.

Ruud Gullit, understandably, was not 100 percent fit after a succession of knee operations in the past year. Striker Marco van Basten had lost confidence, Ronald Koeman had not had a happy first season with Barcelona, while the versatile Frank Rijkaard was criticized for his work habits.

They were called the Orange without the Juice, the Clockwork Orange that was not ticking properly. Most simply felt that cream had to rise to the top sooner or later.

Ireland's critics were delighted that the Republic ran into a team even more boring than it in the second match. Egypt made it plain that it would do anything to win a point but its time–wasting tactics ruined the game.

At times one had the impression that Egypt goalkeeper Ahmed Shobeir thought the ball was his own personal property as he was reluctant to let anyone else play with it.

The inevitable 0–0 score prompted Charlton to say: "I have never seen a team with so little ambition (as Egypt). They did not have one shot at our goal. I despise this type of football and their time–wasting."

ABOVE / *Ireland's Kevin Sheedy (No. 11) infiltrates a swarm of Egyptian defenders and seems to have a wide-open net ahead of him. The shot failed, though certainly not through lack of effort from the flying Irishman.*
David Jacobs / Action Images

As every game in the group had ended in a draw, there was the possibility that lots would be required to separate the four teams if the third games ended in draws.

England's 1–0 win over Egypt made it group winner, but as Ireland and the Netherlands drew 1–1, they had to draw lots to decide which finished in second and third places. Egypt, with two points, finished at the bottom.

The Republic enjoyed the luck of the Irish when the lots were drawn. It finished second and would play Romania in the second phase. The Netherlands, as third–place team, had to face mighty West Germany, which beat the Dutch in the 1974 World Cup final, 2–1.

There was evidence that some of the Dutch superstars were improving during the game in Palermo. Gullit, running more freely than before, scored a superb opening goal, showing the sort of control and finishing that had made him arguably the most complete footballer in the world.

The three favorites had eventually progressed but not without a few problems. Egypt won two points, many new admirers and, with Cameroon, showed that the gap between Africa and the established soccer powers of Europe and South America is narrowing. ■

Christopher Davies

A RESPECTABLE DISPLAY

E gypt, in its first appearance in the World Cup since 1934, failed to win a game in Italia '90 but won the admiration of the world. With Cameroon, it furthered the cause of African football.

The Egyptians played uncomplicated football, doing the basic things correctly.

Egypt's main weakness was inexperience. It drew 1–1 with the Netherlands, 0–0 with Ireland and lost 1–0 to England. Its coach, Mohammed El–Gohary, affectionately but confusingly called "The Captain" by Egyptians, would surely have settled for that at the start of the tournament.

In their game against the Netherlands, the Egyptians played some superb one–touch football, finding teammates with ease and denying the Dutch space. Players such as defender Hany Ramzy, midfielder Magdy Abed El–Ghani and striker Hossam Hassan were among the best of the first round.

Egypt was well prepared, having been in a training camp for six months. Physically, Egypt lacked nothing. The heat of Palermo and Cagliari was to its liking and in strength and stamina the Egyptians more than matched their opponents.

Italia '90 was a learning process for Egypt, a stepping stone. The Egyptians will realize that, like all teams, they need to improve, most notably defending at the far post. Their displays underlined that Africa's representatives must now be given the respect afforded to those from Europe and South America. ■

Christopher Davies

RIGHT / *Those who thought Egypt would be over its head at the World Cup were mistaken. Though placed into an extremely competitive group, the Egyptians allowed just two goals over three games, and only a 1-0 loss to England prevented these upstarts, making their first World Cup appearance in 56 years, from advancing to the second round.* David Jacobs / Action Images

ABOVE / *David Platt of England receives a pinpoint-accurate pass over his shoulder from Paul Gascoigne and in a single motion hooks it into the Belgian net for a spectacular goal . . .*

. . . that is cause for the pure joy he radiates here. Platt's opportunistic play came in the 119th minute, one minute before the second-round match was headed for penalty kicks. The goal lifted England to the quarterfinals after a game solidly dominated by Belgium. David Jacobs / Action Images

second round EARLY SHOWDOWNS

F IFA had mixed emotions about the makeup of the second round, the pleasure of seeing Cameroon and Costa Rica countered by the fact that first–round favorite USSR had been eliminated.

The success of Cameroon and Costa Rica, plus impressive displays by Egypt and, ultimately, the United States, pleased João Havelange, the FIFA president who was instrumental in increasing the size of the competition from 16 to 24 nations in 1986.

Indeed, the impact that Cameroon and Cost Rica made in Italy prompted one critic to name the tournament the Third World Cup.

Havelange's presidential campaign has been conducted on the back of the emerging countries, although the Africans have done so well over the past three World Cups that they can no longer be called up and coming.

Africa could justifiably claim to be an established power, worthy of rubbing shoulders with the big guns from Europe and South America. Cameroon, particularly, was the latest of the continent's success stories.

Happy as Havelange was at the progress of the less fashionable teams, he would have been dismayed that the second–round draw meant that four of the pre World Cup favorites were to play each other so early in the competition — Argentina and Brazil, the Netherlands and West Germany.

The USSR, runner–up in the 1988 European Championships, had already gone home, victim again of refereeing decisions by the Swede Erik Fredriksson who was blamed for allowing two "offside" goals in the 1986 game against Belgium, which the Soviets lost.

In Italy, Fredriksson failed to notice another Hand of God act by Diego Maradona, who stopped what appeared to be a certain Soviet goal in typical style. The Hand of the Devil would be a more apt phrase.

It was no consolation that Fredriksson was also going home, but having seen one country with a strong tradition depart, FIFA was hoping more would not follow in the USSR's wake.

The second round was a mixture of football at its best and worst; at its most breathtaking and most numbingly tedious.

ABOVE / *Jürgen Klinsmann (No. 18), who has already swapped his jersey, embraces teammate Guido Buchwald after West Germany's 2-1 second-round victory over neighbor and bitter rival the Netherlands at Milan. Though emotions ran deep and as hot as the weather at gametime, the two nations combined to present one of the best matches of the tournament.* David Jacobs / Action Images

The game of the round, and arguably the tournament, was West Germany against the Netherlands, a repeat of the 1974 World Cup final. Once again the Germans won, 2–1, but not without incident and further examples of inadequate refereeing, this time by Juan Loustau of Argentina.

While everyone wants to see cynical foul play punished appropriately, too often officials refereed to the letter of the law rather than the spirit of the rules. They hid behind their cards, possibly thinking "that probably looked like a foul to FIFA officials in the tribune."

Soccer's ruling body with its hard–line approach had put a huge amount of pressure on the referees; some could handle it, others handed out cards like confetti.

Loustau sent off Rudi Völler, the West German striker who had, a minute earlier, been involved in an incident with the Netherlands midfielder Frank Rijkaard.

Rijkaard spat three times at Völler — violent conduct — and was correctly shown the red card. But after the initial incident

Völler had done his best to avoid contact with Dutch goalkeeper Hans van Breukelen, which he virtually did.

Shamefully, Loustau sent off Völler in what the world's press called a dreadful decision.

Loustau was to later book Lothar Matthäus, the German captain, for time-wasting. In fact, the Germans had taken a quick free kick and Matthäus put the ball in the net, not realizing play had not been officially started. The decision was as inexplicable as the dismissal of Völler.

Despite being reduced to 10 men, the two teams put on a display of football of the highest order. The game probably came one contest too early for the Netherlands, which had given glimpses of the poise that made the Dutch such stylists.

West Germany was predictable — predictably impressive — but the tournament was appearing to be woefully short of real stars and real flair.

Argentina, not surprisingly, relied heavily on Maradona, who had been magnificent despite the burden of an ankle injury that demanded rest. That would come but there were more urgent matters — like the defense of the World Cup.

The defending champions were outplayed by their traditional rival, but Brazil was beset by hard luck in the goalmouth.

Argentina rode its luck, took everything Brazil had to offer on the jaw and then delivered the sucker punch.

Inevitably, it was Maradona who supplied the moment of inspiration it took to win the game. His surging run attracted the attention of three Brazilian players, leaving Claudio Caniggia free. At the crucial moment, Maradona slipped the ball to Caniggia who beat goalie Claudio Taffarel with a low shot with just eight minutes remaining.

Argentina may have been the luckiest team in the world — it was something, no doubt, Brazil pondered during its long flight home. Brazil had wasted too many chances while Maradona had proved, as if he needed to, that he is still the most gifted player in the world, bad ankle or not.

Strikers such as Marco van Basten (the Netherlands), Toni Polster (Austria) and Gary Lineker (England), of whom so much was expected, had generally been disappointments.

Instead, the world was talking about Roger Milla, a 38-year-old striker from Cameroon, who had twice retired but had been brought back onto the squad via government intervention.

Milla was enjoying a quiet life playing low-grade soccer on Réunion Island in the Indian Ocean when the call came.

Milla's two goals against Colombia put him atop the scoring charts with Spain's Míchel (Miguel González), who had also scored four times.

Another unlikely name, Salvatore Schillaci, had also dominated the headlines since coming on as a substitute and scoring in Italy's opening game against Austria.

The Sicilian, known simply as Totò, scored again in the 2–0 win over Uruguay. In a matter of months, Schillaci had gone from being on the brink of not making the squad to his country's most popular player.

The second round was generally disappointing. Dragan Stojković finally produced his best form to inspire Yugoslavia to a 2–1 win over Spain in a yawn of a game; Ireland, not surprisingly, needed penalties to dispose of Romania; Belgium dominated the match against England yet lost, 1–0, (shades of Argentina vs Brazil); and Czechoslovakia ended Costa Rica's dreams, 4–1.

The general feeling was that there were as many good teams going home as were advancing to the third round. ■

Christopher Davies

SPECTACULAR SEQUEL

WEST GERMANY 2 NETHERLANDS 1. *Milan, June 24*

The Dutch have never forgotten nor forgiven the Germans for stealing the 1974 World Cup from Johan Cruyff's super team, and when the two nations met again in the semifinals of the 1988 European Championships, some of the Dutch players had no qualms about using the word 'hate' to describe their feelings for their arch-enemy.

Fate added fuel to the flames by setting the revenge match in Milan. In the Lombardian capital, Dutch aces Ruud Gullit, Marco van Basten and Frank Rijkaard top the bill for European champs AC Milan while the German trio of Lothar Matthäus, Andreas Brehme and Jürgen Klinsmann are the stars of mortal rivals Inter Milan.

Feelings ran so high that on the weekend of the game the Dutch authorities ordered various border posts between the two countries to be closed, for fear of incidents.

With the thermometer reading 86 degrees on a humid summer night and with a wall-to-wall atmosphere built up by 75,000 fans, the scene was set for a long, hard battle. The first blood was drawn in an incident started in the 21st minute. Dutch central defender Rijkaard fouled Rudolf Völler and the German forward added some topspin to his fall. It was enough for the Argentine referee to flourish the yellow card in Rijkaard's face, and for the Dutchman then to spit in Völler's while they were waiting for the free kick. Völler's reaction earned him a yellow card, and when the move ended with Völler colliding with Dutch goalie Hans van Breukelen, it was enough to provoke more

ABOVE / *Jürgen Klinsmann of West Germany grimaces as the ball is stripped away from him on a sliding tackle by the Netherlands' Adri Van Tiggelen during the intense second-round match.* David Jacobs / Action Images

THE DIKE BURST

T he Netherlands, whose preparations for major competitions invariably seem to be disrupted by a crisis, became victim of its internal wrangling and fizzled in Italia '90.

Player complaints by the 1988 European champions meant that coach Thijs Libregts, who had guided the Netherlands through the qualifying process, was ousted just weeks before Italia '90.

The majority of players wanted former captain Johan Cruyff, now with Barcelona, as the new coach. Instead, Leo Beenhakker of Ajax was given the temporary and near impossible job of leading the Dutch in the World Cup.

The dissatisfaction on the squad was apparent and the performances had none of the sparkle normally associated with the Dutch.

Marco van Basten, called the best striker in the world, was a shadow of his former self.

Ronald Koeman looked sluggish while Frank Rijkaard, sent off against West Germany for spitting, didn't like playing in defense and it showed.

Ruud Gullit, still recovering from a series of knee operations, is excluded from any criticism. Even at 80 percent of his capabilities, he was the Netherlands' best player both in skill and attitude.

The Netherlands was given a shock in its 1–1 draw against Egypt, was fortunate to draw 0–0 with England, and while it improved in the 1–1 draw against Ireland, the Dutch never looked like the potential finalists many thought they would be. ∎

Christopher Davies

RIGHT / *Colorful Ruud Gullit of the Netherlands is one of the world's best players, but his performance at the World Cup didn't live up to billing. Recent injuries and perhaps his manager's conservative style slowed him to one goal in four games and helped hasten his team's quiet exit from the tournament after the round of 16 without winning a single match (they tied three).*
Daniel Motz / MOTZSPORTS

harsh words, another dose of saliva from Rijkaard and red cards for both protagonists. Rijkaard, normally a peaceful mortal, later apologized, while the Germans unsuccessfully appealed against the red card which was to ban Völler from the next game.

After the duo had seen red, the match became exciting enough to provoke suggestions that soccer would benefit from being permanently reduced to 10 a team.

Beforehand, the war had seemed likely to hinge on the results of individual battles. Gullit–Berthold, Van Basten–Kohler, Winter–Matthäus, Rijkaard–Klinsmann and Van Aerle–Völler. With the big names so tightly marked it was left to the bit actors to deliver the telling lines. The Netherlands' Aron Winter, the 18th player used by coach Leo Beenhakker in four games and one of four desperation changes in a disastrously off-form Dutch team, missed easy chances in the 7th and 8th minutes which could have changed the course of the game, and teammate Jan Wouters squandered three more.

The two squads traded punches until Klinsmann punished the Dutch in the 51st minute. The German forward, operating solo since Völler's dismissal, had produced a performance he described as the best of his career. His close control and devastating sprinting, with his blonde mane billowing in the slipstream, had been poison for the Dutch defense. It was his left foot that converted an excellent cross from the impressive Guido Buchwald, a one–man panzer force whom coach Franz Beckenbauer later named as his player of the tournament.

To rub salt into wounds, another Inter Milan player, Brehme, scored Germany's second goal four minutes from full-time. The left–back used his 'wrong' right foot to curl a shot past Van Breukelen from the very corner of the penalty area. The Dutch were so dejected that even when Ronald Koeman scored from the penalty spot in the 89th minute, they made less than

ABOVE / *Thomas Hässler is one of West Germany's better-known weapons; his speed from the midfield is credited with opening up numerous opportunities for his prolific-scoring teammates.*
David Jacobs / Action Images

half–hearted attempts to rush back for the equalizer.

Dutch misery was typified by two-time European Player of the Year Marco van Basten. His timing was so grotesquely off that, even when the Germans failed to take the ball from him, he somehow managed to trip over it. When the final whistle sounded he shook no hands, exchanged no shirts. Raising a limp arm toward the Dutch fans, he walked head–down and disconsolately silent toward the dressing rooms. He and the Dutch were out, Van Basten without scoring a goal and the Netherlands without winning a match. ∎

Graham Turner

MARCONI
AND
SPAGHETTI

Bologna, which hosted Colombia, Yugoslavia and the United Arab Emirates in the first round, may not have been a focal point of the 1990 World Cup but the city, set in the spectacular Apennine Hills, is rich in tradition and history.

It is because of one of its former inhabitants that millions of people could follow the progress of Italia '90 — Marconi, the inventor of the wireless, was born there.

Six of its sons have gone on to become Pope, Gregory XIII, reformer of the calendar, among them.

However, the city is best known for its cuisine, which is the most famous in Italy. Tagliatelle (or spaghetti) bolognese, tortellini and lasagna all originate from Bologna and these foods are invariably supplemented by a glass of Lambrusco, the regional wine.

Apart from its gastronomy, Bologna, which is notoriously left wing in its politics, is a business and industrial center set in the heart of Italy's thriving north.

The city has a long and varied history, which includes 300 years as a papal state. In 1814 it was occupied by the British in support of the Austrians against Napoleon.

Bologna was one of the eight sites used for the 1934 World Cup and although the Stadio dall'Ara has changed since then, locals say it still retained its soul.

In the second round, Bologna hosted England's 1–0 extra–time win over Belgium, and the city that had promoted a message of non–violence was spared the excesses that shamed the English supporters elsewhere. ∎

Christopher Davies

ABOVE / *The three first-round match-ups in Bologna provided little potential for fan trouble, but authorities there still took no chances, posting alert, well-armed police, and plenty of them. They were well prepared by Bologna's final game — a more dangerous second-round pairing of Belgium and England.* David Jacobs / Action Images

OPPOSITE / *Low-key, unassuming Bologna basked in the golden glow of four World Cup matches. The north-central Italian metropolis of a half million shared first-round hosting responsibilities of Group D with Milan.* courtesy of ENIT–SF

Bologna

ABOVE / *Disbelieving En-glishmen mob David Platt af-ter his dramatic goal in the final minute of extra time de-feated Belgium.* David Jacobs / Action Images

"After dominating the whole game, losing in that way was hellish," complained Enzo Scifo. "We produced our best performance of the tournament and lost unjustly," moaned Stephane Demol. "We just ran out of luck, but at least we can go home with our heads held high and proud of having played some good soccer," commented coach Guy Thys.

The remarks, which could have been applied to so many games in this World Cup, emanated from a distressed Belgian team that had been cruelly beaten in the very last minute of extra time by a superbly opportunistic goal from England's hero of the night, David Platt.

The timid 24–year–old Aston Villa forward had been Robson's choice to replace Steve McMahon in midfield after 72 minutes. McMahon himself had joined the team as a replacement for skipper Bryan Robson, sent home with an Achilles tendon injury two days earlier. But Platt surfaced just in time to decide a closely–fought absorbing contest when the 35,000 crowd was already anticipating a penalty shootout.

Paul Gascoigne, once again England's key performer, was midway into Belgian territory and ready to take a short free kick until frenzied shouting from the England bench persuaded him to chip the ball into the penalty area. There, Platt turned away from the Belgian markers and, as the ball dropped over his shoulder, hooked it past a startled Michel Preud'homme into the far corner of the net.

Belgian coach Guy Thys decided on a defensive game plan with a 4–5–1 formation which, in hindsight, was conservative enough to be his ultimate undoing.

The Belgian defense kept England on such a tight rein that the only appreciable chance was a goal scored by John Barnes who timed a Gary Lineker cross into the Belgian net only to see

ABOVE / *Steve Bull of England (No. 21) is a little more on target than his Belgian opponent in a lively moment from the sparkling second-round match–up.* Daniel Motz / MOTZSPORTS

ANOTHER HARD LUCK STORY

T he Red Devils of Belgium were just one of the many hard luck stories generated by this World Cup. The last–gasp elimination by England was a cruel recompense for a team that played some of the more attractive soccer of the tournament.

Leading the charge were two men — one, a coach brought back from retirement, and the other, a young player reborn.

Guy Thys had decided to retire in 1989 after 12 years as coach of the Red Devils, leading them to the European Championship final in 1980 and a creditable fourth place in the Mexico World Cup. His successor, 39–year–old Walter Meeuws, was a victim of player discontent and lasted only eight months. So, back, at 67, came Thys.

His elder statesman approach again smoothed over the traditional tribal wars in the dressing room and got the World Cup show on the road with two impressive wins. The overall evaluation of his work was so positive that he was immediately asked to stay for another two years.

The reborn athlete who provided the spark on the field was midfield player Enzo Scifo. The Belgians had nationalized Italian–born Scifo in 1984. Three years later he succumbed to the lure of Italy, joined Inter Milan and took his family home. Scifo failed — so badly that he was farmed out to French club Bordeaux. He failed again. In 1989, Guy Roux, coach of shoestring club Auxerre, decided to give Scifo another chance. Scifo did well enough to reclaim his place on the Red Devils, but then argued with Meeuws and was banned. Back came Thys, back came Scifo, and in Italy the 24–year–old midfielder showed why he had been regarded as a teenage prodigy. ■

Graham Turner

RIGHT / *Bruno Versavel and Belgium flew through the first round with the greatest of ease — except for a 2 — 1 loss to Spain. Were it not for a last — minute goal by England, the Belgians' crowd — pleasing style of soccer might have sailed farther.* David Jacobs / Action Images

linesman Helmut Kohl agitating his flag for offside — one of many much-debated calls by the Austrian official.

Belgium, on the other hand, touched wood twice but failed to convert. In the 14th minute, a good bounce favored Jan Ceulemans after a tackle by Des Walker, and the powerful Brugge player tested the strength of goalie Peter Shilton's post with a left-footed screamer. In the sixth minute of the second half, Scifo did likewise with a memorable 30-yard shot masterfully struck with the outside of the right foot.

By this stage, Scifo and Gascoigne had stamped their dominant personalities on an absorbing match, with Belgium ahead on points. The two were vastly different. The Belgian

ABOVE / *Things get tense in front of Ireland's net as an Ion Andone header nearly scoots past Irish defender Niall Quinn and toward goalkeeper Patrick Bonner. 'Twas no goal for Romania, or in the rest of the match — the game went Ireland's way on penalty kicks.* Daniel Motz / MOTZSPORTS

midfielder, slim, dark, subtle and artistic; the Englishman, solid, busy and gutsy with surprising skill and clarity of ideas.

England, operating a five-man defense with Mark Wright as sweeper for the second time in Robson's eight-year regime, had key players such as Lineker, Walker, Terry Butcher and Wright nursing injuries from game to game and even Gascoigne ran out of gas during the half hour of extra time, when the Belgians looked more resilient. Thys, however, was prepared to die for his conservative principles and even when he sent on the overly-aggressive Nico Claesen, it was not to gamble on an extra forward, but at the expense of Marc De Grijse and simply maintaining the 4-5-1.

The fans in the Dall'Ara Stadium were riding England for wasting time when Belgium was electrocuted by Platt's lightning strike.

Graham Turner

IRELAND 0 ROMANIA 0 (aet). 5–4 on penalties.
Genoa, June 25

David O'Leary had never been the apple of Jack Charlton's eye. Not since he refused to cancel a family vacation and go on summer tour on very short notice in 1986. The Arsenal defender was rapidly swept under the carpet until an injury crisis forced Charlton to recall him for a game in Spain in November 1988. Even then the Irish coach couldn't bring himself to call O'Leary, who had in the meantime added fuel to the flames by dedicating a whole chapter of his autobiography to his rift with Charlton. It was finally the team doctor who grabbed a phone to do the honors.

Fate decreed that, against Romania, O'Leary should emerge from the reserves' bench in the third minute of extra time to take over from the struggling left–back Stephan Staunton. O'Leary slotted smoothly into the unfamiliar role of fullback, and the scoreboard that had never shifted from 0–0 indicated that a place in the quarterfinals was down to penalties.

Kevin Sheedy, Christopher Houghton, Andrew Townsend and Anthony Cascarino all beat the Romanian goalie Silviu Lung. Danut Lupu, Iosif Rotariu and Ionut Lupescu outwitted Patrick Bonner. Then up stepped 22–year–old Dinamo Bucharest rookie Daniel Timofte and Bonner dove low to his right to save. Ireland needed to convert its last kick to win and the man on the hot seat was O'Leary. While his wife back home had to rush into the garden to avoid a nervous breakdown, O'Leary coolly put his kick in the net and Jack Charlton, who before the penalty shootout had told his men he was proud of them whatever the outcome, permitted himself a quiet word of congratulation to his least favorite son.

The Irish thus secured the dubious honor of becoming the first team to reach the World Cup quarterfinals without winning a game and by scoring just two goals. But on balance they were worth their ticket.

It had been suggested that Emerich Ienei's Romanian team was suffering acute distress on account of the serious disturbances in Bucharest. But in the opening exchanges in the Ferraris Stadium, Romania had looked capable of taking the Irish defense apart with ball skills and neatly–played one–twos hinging on Ion Sabau, Michael Klein, Florin Radocioiu and, above all, the so–called 'Maradona of the Carpathians,' Gheorghe Hagi. But Charlton's team, never willing to lay down and die, plugged away with its now familiar long–pass formula and, despite losing attacker John Aldridge through injury as early as the 25th minute, created enough chances to have won the game.

ABOVE / *Patrick Bonner minded the nets admirably for Ireland — yielding just three goals in five games — but he also benefited from a rock-tough, defensive-minded team in front of him.* David Jacobs / Action Images

ROMAN
ROOTS

Thousands of Romanian fans stayed longer than they planned when their team edged its way into the second round. And more than 100 asked for political asylum during their stay, for it was during the first round that the Romanian government called in miners to subdue protests in Bucharest.

Many Romanian players, anxious spectators during the violent overthrow of Nicolae Ceaucescu, looked upon the World Cup as their ticket to fortunes in the West. For decades, soccer federation officials had corrupted the Romanian league by fixing matches, usually those between Bucharest powers Steaua and Dinamo. Ceaucescu and most of his family favored Steaua, sponsored by the army, but his son Valentin preferred Dinamo, run by the Securitate secret police. Following the rebellion, Dinamo changed its name to Unirea in an effort to eradicate all memory of the Securitate's stigma.

Other Eastern European nations had permitted egress by players, but only when they'd reached a minimum age, usually 28 or 30. Romanian players, though, were bound to their domestic clubs for their entire careers.

All such restrictions fell during the political upheavals in Eastern Europe, and Italian clubs were among the first to lure Romanian talent. Midfielder Marius Lacatus of Steaua, scorer of both goals in the 2–0 win over the Soviet Union, signed a contract with Italian club Fiorentina during the tournament. Teammate Florin Radocioiu left Unirea for Bari.

Italy was a fitting site for their coming–out, for it was the Roman Empire that sowed the seeds of civilization and language in Romania — hence the name — during the second century A.D. ∎

Ridge Mahoney

RIGHT / *Gheorghe Hagi and his Romanian teammates did not lose their shirts in the World Cup as they were expected to. The Romanians, underdogs in their group, played well enough to advance to the second round, including an especially satisfying win over the Soviet Union and a tie against eventual runner-up Argentina. Only a second-round loss to Ireland on penalty kicks kept the Romanians' success from passing into the astounding category.*
Cynthia Greer

The cornerstone for Ireland was the sterling work of Paul McGrath, taking pressure off the back four and shoring up a midfield where Townsend, Sheedy and especially Houghton produced very complete performances. Like so many opponents before them, the Romanians were gradually ground down and persuaded that their superior technique was worthless if there was no room to use it. And one department in which the Irish excel is their ability to deny space to their opponents.

Hagi found himself restricted to attempting as many as nine long–range shots, of which only three were on target and none was good enough to beat

ABOVE / *Miss Manners would be horrified as Ireland's Kevin Sheedy (No. 11) cuts in line in front of Romania's Gheorghe Hagi, whose face quite correctly shows indignation over this rude affront.*
David Jacobs / Action Images

OPPOSITE / *Italy's Giuseppe Giannini (left) and Uruguay's Hugo De León provide a brief, well-choreographed moment of grace during their teams' second-round match, won 2–0 by Italy.*
Lehtikuva Oy

the sound Bonner. Three–million–dollar striker Radocioiu was so frustrated by the Irish defense that he was replaced by Lupu in the 70th minute. Charlton's team began to outrun Romania on the flanks and provide crosses which the twin towers, Cascarino and Niall Quinn, could have converted with a little more accuracy in their heading. Quinn, in particular, could have avoided extra time if he had placed his 86th minute effort a fraction lower.

After O'Leary and Bonner had settled the issue during the penalty shootout, local journalists besieged Charlton with questions about Ireland's quarterfinal opponent, none other than Italy. "The only thing on my mind," said the Irish coach with grim seriousness, "is getting back to the hotel and drinking the coldest pint of beer I can find."

Graham Turner

Three victories in three games. No goals conceded. Thus far Italy had won admiration from fans, media and even rival players and coaches for its offense-minded game, its high standard of individual technique, its speed, its positional play and its methods of pressurizing opponents to gain rapid recovery of the ball. Where it hadn't impressed so deeply was in the scoring department, where only Salvatore Schillaci, the little-known Sicilian reserve, had lived up to pre World Cup promo promises.

Uruguay coach Oscar Tabárez decided the antidote was a blotting-paper strategy of absorption and ultimately frustration. Out of his lineup went creative midfielder Rubén Paz, a fine ball artist. In came the hard-working Rubén Pereira. Out went star strikers Rubén Sosa and Antonio Alzamendi. In came the faster Carlos Aguilera and Daniel Fonseca, both better at marking opponents and hiding the ball from them.

For over an hour, Tabárez's stratagem worked. The Sky Blues marked tight, retained possession in short-passing moves and put up road blocks on the supply routes to the Italian attack, already affected by the loss of the talented Milan duo of Roberto Donadoni and Carlo Ancelotti. Giuseppe Giannini was unable to run the show as he would have liked, and newcomer Nicola Berti looked long on legs but short on ideas. Strikers Roberto Baggio and Schillaci continued to look dangerous on the ball, but were rarely able to find it. The Uruguayans were not paranoid about worrying Walter Zenga in the Italian goal. Their prime aim was to rile the hosts by spoiling the party.

By the interval they must have been happy with their performance. The 74,000 fans in the Olympic Stadium were becoming restless and frightened. Their team had burned off large quantities of energy but had rarely been able to build coherent passing movements among the jungle of legs in midfield.

The turning point came eight minutes after the break when Italy coach Azeglio Vicini decided to withdraw the blunt Berti and send in somebody sharper. He chose to offer a gift to Inter Milan forward Aldo Serena, who was celebrating his 30th birthday. Serena is a wandering minstrel among scorers who has played with more clubs than Jack Nicklaus. Unable to hold down a regular first-team place at Inter, he was a surprise choice for the Italian squad.

He decided, however, to accept the birthday invitation with devastating gratitude. Serena had only been in the game for 12 minutes when he latched onto the ball, just right of center on the fringe of the Uruguayan penalty area, and cheekily flicked the ball between

CHANGE
OF
HABITS

Uruguay will be remembered as much for what it didn't do in Italia '90 as for what it did. Uruguayans were noted for their rough tactics in Mexico in 1986 and coach Oscar Washington Tabárez must be congratulated for the change in style.

The Uruguay of 1990 may not have been a supremely gifted team, but there was none of the cynicism that had become associated with the country.

Uruguay arrived as a good bet to reach the second round but probably not much more. Its four games left the impression that Uruguay was lacking in quality players in key areas.

Its opening 0–0 draw with Spain was one of the more predictable results of the World Cup. It was shadow boxing with hardly a punch thrown, but both nations were happy to have avoided defeat.

In its second match, Uruguay came up against a strong–finishing Belgian team. It was a night when Belgium's strikers were at their sharpest and the 3–1 score did not really do Uruguay justice.

The defeat meant Uruguay had to beat South Korea to be assured of a place in the second round. Uruguay was clearly nervous and only a header, scored in the 92nd minute of play, assured Uruguay of advancing.

The good news was that Uruguay had qualified for the next round. The bad news was it would play Italy in Rome. The inevitable news was that Italy won, by a score of 2–0. ∎

Christopher Davies

RIGHT / *Uruguay's Nelson Gutiérrez (No. 2) challenges Emilio Butragueño of Spain. That typifies Uruguay at World Cup '90: it challenged but did not have the firepower to conquer. Uruguay hosted the first World Cup in 1930 and won two championships in the competition's early years, but recently it has slipped into the second rank of world soccer powers.* Daniel Motz / MOTZSPORTS

Nelson Gutiérrez's legs into the path of the charging Schillaci.

Schillaci's left–footed shot in front of Uruguayan goalie Fernando Alvez did its best to force a hole in the top left corner of the net. A micro–second of disbelief and then Schillaci, his teammates, the 74,000 fans and millions of Italian citizens went berserk.

Tabárez, who had already sent on Sosa for Aguilera on the hour–mark, waited 10 minutes before gambling on an offense–minded second change aimed at pushing forward for an equalizer. Off went midfielder Santiago Ostolaza and on came attacker Alzamendi. Within two minutes his gamble had failed and Uruguay was dead and buried. Italy's Giannini floated in a free kick from the right and there was Serena again, beating Gutiérrez to the ball and glancing a header past Alvez.

The Uruguayans, once again disappointingly eliminated with just one agonizing victory and two goals to show for four games, opted to lay the blame at the door of English referee George Courtney, whom they accused of being a homer. The British Embassy in Montevideo received three bomb threats, and Courtney did not officiate again during the World Cup. ∎

Graham Turner

MARADONA'S MIRACLE

ARGENTINA 1 BRAZIL 0. *Turin, June 24*

No matter how many times the Brazilians review the tape of their fateful 90 minutes, they will never understand how they lost. "We were lucky," Diego Maradona had the good grace to admit afterward. "The only explanation is that God was on our side."

When the final whistle sounded, Maradona went to console Careca (Antonio Oliveira), his teammate at Napoli. "We played our best soccer of the tournament," complained the Brazilian. "We dominated 89 of the 90 minutes. We let Maradona go free once, and we paid a big price."

The match was all about Brazil. Coach Sebastião Lazaroni stuck to his usual team and his much–criticized system. Ironically, it produced flowing soccer of a quality hitherto unseen in the tournament and which was later sadly missed. Minute 1: Argentine goalie Sergio Goycochea is lucky to deflect a Careca shot for a corner. Minute 2: shot from Alemão (Ricardo Brito). Minute 4: shot from Alemão. Minute 5: shot from Müller (Luiz Costa). And so it continued until the excellent Branco (Claudio Leal) broke free on the left in the 17th minute and his cross was headed against the post by Dunga (Carlos Verri), playing a more offense–minded role than he had done during the first phase.

OPPOSITE (top) / *Goalie Sergio Goycochea (No. 12) of Argentina is challenged by Brazil's high–flying Ricardo Rocha. Though besieged by Brazilian scoring opportunities all during the match, none went past the harried netminder . . .*

(bottom) / *. . . and while Brazil's Alemão, here darting between Claudio Caniggia (No. 8) and Ricardo Giusti (No. 14), and his teammates worked doggedly to attack the Argentine net, they always came up short.* Steve Hale / Action Images

ABOVE (top) / *Pow! Bang! Zap! Boom! Brazil peppered the Argentine net with shots. Here Careca, though rushed by Pedro Monzón of Argentina, strikes a solid header from close–in, aiming it to the upper–right corner of the net . . .*

(bottom) / *. . . but, as would be Brazil's maddening lot all through the match, this one sailed just past the post.* Steve Hale / Action Images

A SOUR SAMBA

B efore the World Cup, very few would have predicted that Brazil would not reach the last eight of a tournament it was a favorite to win. The early departure of the three–time champs was astonishing. Brazil outplayed, outclassed and all but humiliated world champion Argentina, but wasted so many good plays that one late moment of magic from Diego Maradona was enough to send the team back to Rio.

Brazil's World Cup strategy was questionable. The Brazilians decided to break a 20–year World Cup drought by naming chunky ex–goalie Sebastião Lazaroni as coach. He, in turn, decided that to win in Rome one had to do as the Europeans do. He thus molded his team with players based in Europe and made sweeping changes to traditional styles and concepts. Instead of a flat back four, he brought in a sweeper; placed two central defenders in front of him; and strengthened the midfield area. That left just three players to create the sort of attacking, happy–go–lucky soccer that Brazilians eat, drink and base their dances on.

Lazaroni's Common Market team provoked schizophrenia in Brazil. Ex–megastar Zico, now Secretary of State for Sport, demanded that emigrants be banned from the national team.

With the loss to Argentina, the dam of resentment burst. Lazaroni, criticized, vilified and all but charged with high treason for the destruction of values held sacred, fled the country having, fortunately, already found work — inevitably — in Europe. ■

Graham Turner

RIGHT / *This Brazilian supporter is inconsolable long after the end of her team's heart-rending loss to Argentina. Brazil brought a team capable of winning the World Cup, but it exited, like several others, shaking heads in puzzlement at the bizarre twists of fate in this tournament, and wondering: How could we so thoroughly outplay an opponent and still lose?* Luigi Baldelli / AC

At this stage it required no tactical expert to make sense of a one–way game. Brazil's fullbacks, Jorginho (Jorge Campos) and Branco were surging forward on the flanks. Valdo Candido was decorating the play with some beautifully creative touches. Careca and Müller were creating problems for the overworked Argentine defense. Alemão and Dunga were exerting so much pressure in midfield that practically all the play was confined to Argentine territory. And Maradona was simply crowded out.

Argentina's first goal attempt was a limp shot from Pedro Troglio after 26 minutes. The underlying violence that has traditionally characterized confrontations between the two South American rivals soon started to bubble to the surface, with Argentina's Pedro Monzón and Ricardo Giusti and then Brazil's Ricardo Rocha all cautioned by the French referee in a turbulent spell before the interval.

The gods dealt Brazil yet another bad hand in the 53rd minute when Careca broke free on the left and crashed a shot against the post. The rebound headed for Alemão who also slammed the ball against the woodwork.

After an hour Argentine coach Carlos Bilardo added more cohesion to his midfield by replacing Troglio with Gabriel Calderón, and while Brazil was still squandering chance after chance, Argentina confirmed in the 80th minute the old adage so often expressed by one of the country's most famous footballing sons, Alfredo di Stéfano: "Goals are not deserved," he insists, "they are scored."

The travesty of justice was consummated thanks to a moment of genius from Maradona — Argentina's only hope. He picked up a pass midway into the Brazilian half, sucked three Brazilians toward him and deceived them all by threading a masterly pass to an unmarked Claudio Caniggia, who neatly sidestepped goalie Claudio Taffarel and chipped the ball into the net.

With the Brazilians throwing themselves forward in kamikaze attacks, they suffered another blow five minutes before the end when Ricardo Gomes felled Argentina's José Basualdo as he headed on a solo run towards Taffarel, and was expelled. Lazaroni then made two red–alert changes and Müller had one last golden chance to score in the 88th minute. As with every single one of the previous chances, it failed to arrive in the net, and injustice was finally done.

Many of the Brazilians left the field in tears, with sweeper Mauro Galvão later bitterly, and none too sportingly, slamming Alemão for failing to flatten Maradona in the three–on–one situation, which had led to the Argentine goal, and insinuating that he had been too kind on his Napoli teammate.

OPPOSITE (top) / *Soccer fans
learn their colors early: This
young man took his Brazilian
green, yellow and blue home
much earlier than he wanted
to . . .* Luigi Baldelli / AC

(bottom) / *. . . while this
young beauty carried her
multi-blue hues of Argentina
all the way to the final match.*
Roberto Koch / AC

Lazaroni could only say, "I challenge anybody to find a logical explanation for this result. Our luck just ran out."

For the Argentine team that had yet to reach even the minimum level expected of world champions, the miracle result was seen as the gigantic injection of morale that was so desperately needed. "We have defeated a great team," claimed a radiant Bilardo. "Now we fear nobody."

Graham Turner

THE CZECH CYCLONE

CZECHOSLOVAKIA 4 COSTA RICA 1.
Bari, June 23

The 'Czech Cyclone,' Tomas Skuhravý, finally brought the Costa Ricans down from cloud nine with a hat-trick of headers. They were enough to take the tall, powerful center-forward to the head of the World Cup scoring charts, after his double strike against the United States, and to earn him a handsome contract with Italian club Genoa.

Only 20,000 fans turned up at the Nuovo Comunale Stadium to watch a match that produced five of the 18 goals scored in the second round. No one in Costa Rica was churlish enough to point accusing fingers at any of the World Cup heroes who had written history for the tiny Central American nation. But high on the list of

ABOVE / *Teams, such as
Czechoslovakia here, found a
good way to get "psyched up"
for the tough match ahead
was to seek encouragement
from loyal boosters.* Jon Van
Woerden

excuses for such a conclusive defeat was the absence of goalkeeper Luis Gabelo Conejo, the foundation stone of the first-phase successes, who had failed to recover from an injury sustained during the victory over Sweden. His understudy, 'Panther' (Hermidio) Barrantes, weighed in with some excellent reflex saves but was far from commanding against the serial bombardment tactic adopted by Czech coach Jozef Vengloš.

The semi-pros of Costa Rica once again acquitted themselves with dignity during the first hour of a match amply dominated by a Czech team that reinforced the favorable impression it had created during the first phase. Its supremacy was based on strength and speed, and when the lofty Skuhravý scored the first of his three goals by heading home a Lubomír Moravčík cross as early as the 11th minute, Costa Rica appeared to be against the ropes and ripe for a devastating knockout.

The Czechs, however, eased off the gas, as if overconfidently expecting a

NINETY-DAY MIRACLE

Things may never be the same in this Central American country with a population of 2–1/2 million following the historic feat of reaching the last 16 in Italy.

Four coaches were involved in bringing the feat to pass — first, Gustavo de Simone; then to a tandem formed by the Spaniard Antonio Moyano and home–based Marvin Rodríguez; and finally, Yugoslav–born Velibor 'Bora' Milutinovic.

It was Milutinovic who led Mexico to the quarterfinals in 1986 and then did the same with Costa Rica after Moyano and Rodríguez departed. It all began with a phone call from Costa Rica soccer federation supremo Isaac Sasso, who had failed in bids to hire Argentine coaches Omar Sivori and César Luis Menotti. Bora accepted a 90–day contract worth $12,000 per month. "Not for the money," he was at pains to point out, "but to be involved in the World Cup. I am a soccer gypsy," he laughed.

The 48–year–old polyglot cultivates a devil–may–care exterior and conceals the secrets of his impressive track record. Amid accusations of a frivolous approach to the job, he took the squad by the scruff of the neck. Out went big names like forwards Leonni Flores and Evaristo Coronado. In came nobodies like fullback Ronald González, a reserve at Saprissa.

"Everyone told me I was mad," he said. "I would have liked to play open, attacking soccer, but Costa Rica is condemned to defense — absorb the opposition's play and counter-attack.

"I was lucky to find players capable of putting my ideas into practice. It worked." ∎

Graham Turner

LEFT / *Soccer player-become-contortionist Hector Marchena typifies the kind of effort given by Costa Rica at World Cup '90. Expected to be solidly drummed from the tournament after the first round, the Costa Ricans instead rang up victories over Scotland and Sweden. Though suffering a crushing second-round loss to Czechoslovakia, the players returned to their tiny country as heroes.*
Sven Simon / Lehtikuva Oy

handsome victory to be a mere formality, and it wasn't until Roger Flores, Claudio Jara and Juan Cayasso had posed problems for Jan Stejskal in the Czech goal that they decided to get the show back on the road.

Trailing by a single goal at the interval, Costa Rica's coach Bora Milutinovic decided to send on Miracle Man Hernán Medford for the whole of the second half instead of the half-hour customarily allotted to him. After 12 minutes the gamble seemed to have paid off. Midfielder Oscar Ramírez floated in a free kick from the right and defender Ronald González showed he, too, was in the Skuhravý class by putting a violently struck header past Stejskal.

The Czechs, however, had the good fortune to regain their lead after six minutes of disconcerted play. The Costa Rican defense hesitated in clearing the ball, and Jozef Chovanec moved in, headed the ball to Skuhravý, who, in turn, headed it in for his second goal.

"I don't understand why," said Milutinovic, "but we crumbled after that second goal." Costa Rica inexplicably threw in the towel.

Luboš Kubík was allowed to score the third goal with a free kick impeccably bent into the angle between the crossbar and post in the 76th minute, and six minutes later Skuhravý was allowed to complete his hat-trick by outleaping González once again at a corner.

The Czechs, initially rated as rank outsiders and labeled as very much an average central European team, had once again looked a strong, technically accomplished team. The team's strength relied on an effective midfield balance of Kubík, who seemed to have gained in quality since his move to Italian club Fiorentina, and Chovanec, who displayed some cultured left-footed skills and creative ability. The inclusion of two more talented left-footers, Moravčík and Ivo Knoflíček, raised questions of compatibility, and the most potentially damaging flaw in the team's collective character was its petulance and habit of committing unnecessary fouls. Even in this game, where the Czech's superiority was never seriously questioned, there were yellow cards for Jan Kocian, Ivan Hašek and František Straka.

The Costa Ricans strolled amiably out of the tournament having amply surpassed all expectations and headed for a heroes' welcome back in San José. Milutinovic, their 'smiling gypsy' of a coach, bade a grateful adios to the Costa Rican team and headed home to Mexico to resume work with his club team. ■

Graham Turner

RIGHT / *It's experience over youth this time as 38-year-old Roger Milla of Cameroon swerves around Colombia's 23-year-old daredevil goalie, René Higuita, who had come out to challenge. Milla scored, then scored again just two minutes later to swing the second-round game to Cameroon.* David Jacobs / Action Images

THE MANE EVENT

C olombian soccer made headlines for all the wrong reasons after it qualified for Italia '90. In November 1989, league play was suspended after referee Alvaro Ortega was murdered, allegedly for failing to favor Medellin — one of four Colombian clubs said to be controlled by drug cartels — in its match against America.

A couple of months later, Colombians voted their team's qualification for the World Cup as the biggest domestic news story of the year, placing the murder of President Viriglio Barco Vargas second and the drug wars third.

Only once before — in eight attempts — had Colombia reached the World Cup, in 1962, and that appearance ended in the first round with a 5–0 loss to Yugoslavia.

Prior to Italia '90, most headlines about the Colombian team heralded the drug wars and the "Hairdo Duo" — orange–maned midfielder Carlos Valderamma and roving goalkeeper René Higuita with the long black curls. It was Valderamma who set up Freddy Rincón for a tying goal in the last minute of Colombia's group finale against eventual champ West Germany. The goal launched Rincón into Colombian history and the team into the second round.

In the game against Cameroon, Colombia's flamboyant sweeperkeeper was finally caught off-guard. Roger Milla plucked the ball off Higuita, 40 yards out from the goal, and pushed it into the vacated net. Higuita chased him futilely, accepted the criticism and, in typical fashion, refused to change his daredevil style.

That goal and another one, also by Milla, sent Colombia home, but they left behind colorful moments and the impression of a fun–loving team able the handle the pressures of the game and the consequences of their actions. ∎

Ridge Mahoney

LEFT / *In a tournament dominated by teams playing not to lose, Colombia's flashy, aggressive style was a breath of fresh air — they were as colorful as their tri–hued jerseys. Along the way the Colombians managed a tie with eventual champion West Germany, and had they not run into the magic of Roger Milla and Cameroon, the world might have witnessed the development of a new South American power.* David Jacobs / Action Images

François Omam Biyik (No. 7) of Cameroon and Colombia's Andrés Escobar jump to action in pursuit of a loose ball sliding toward the Colombian corner. David Jacobs / Action Images

Genova

HOME
OF
COLUMBUS

enoa looks out to the azure sea draped by steep green hills of the Ligurian Apennines. It's a scene that repeatedly inspires.

Alexander Dumas called it "something unbelievably beautiful." Mark Twain, Henry James, Charles Dickens all arrived at this Mediterranean doorstep. Dickens pronounced it "splendid" and stayed for a year.

As Italy's largest seaport, Genoa boasts a rich seafaring heritage. When the Saracens invaded the port town in 934 A.D., the Genoese responded by building a new fleet and trounced the intruders, pushing them back as far as Constantinople. So began its seafaring legacy, which climaxed in the 16th and 17th centuries when Genoa, known as "La Superba," rivaled Venice as the richest sea-trading center in Italy. Today, the many *palazzi* (palaces), spread throughout the city center, pay homage to the commercial wealth of Genoa's seafaring genius and the intense, often ludicrous, material rivalry of the Genoese and the Venetians.

That Christopher Columbus is one of the most illustrious sons is not something Genoa lets one easily forget. It was, of course, Genoese bankers who financed the expedition of 1492. The airport — built on land reclaimed from the sea — bears the explorer's namesake and celebrations are being planned for the 500th anniversary of Columbus' epic voyage.

Genoa, which hosted the first-round games of Group C along with Turin and the quarterfinal match between Romania and Ireland, is home to soccer rivals Sampdoria and Genoa. Sampdoria greeted the World Cup in 1990 by winning the prestigious Cup Winner's Cup for the first time in history. ■

LEFT / *Genoa, gateway to the Italian Riviera, is always kissed by the Ligurian Sea. Here the city is also being painted by a rare, romantic brush —   winter.* Lucas / Lehtikuva Oy

ABOVE / *Carlos Estrada's reputation as one of the sport's best ball dribblers precedes him, thus the Colombian often must carry extra baggage as he tries to move the ball upfield, as here against Cameroon.* David Jacobs / Action Images

It was bound to happen sooner or later. And destiny decreed that two of the competition's most colorful characters should decide this match in the third minute of the second period of extra time.

In the Colombian goal is the extravagant, flamboyant idol of the nation, René Higuita, the ex–center forward who adds a new dimension to goalkeeping by refusing to accept solitary confinement in the penalty area and frequently races out and joins in the soccer his teammates are playing.

Bearing down on Higuita is Cameroon's Roger Milla, the idol plucked from retirement on the island of Réunion in the Indian Ocean and, at the ripe old age of 38, flown to Italy to make history in every game he plays.

Higuita, 15 yards outside his area, and with no teammates covering his back, sees Milla coming and decides to fool him with a fancy flick of the ball behind the other leg. But Milla has been around too long to be fooled by 23–year–old rookies. With a flourish worthy of a streetwise pickpocket, Milla whips the ball away and, with Higuita desperately lunging after him in a race toward goal, has time to look left and right before grinning, side–footing the ball into the unguarded net and going off to perform the lambada with a corner flag.

"People have been waiting years for me to make a howler like that," said the rueful Colombian goalie afterward. "But I do not intend to change my style of play for anybody."

Higuita's generosity allowed Milla to repeat the feat he had performed against Romania eight days earlier — to make a triumphant second–half entry and score two decisive goals.

Cameroon's Soviet coach Valeri Nepomniatchi decided to play his offensive weapon in the 55th minute in place of midfielder Louis M'Fede. This

ABOVE / *Colombia's Andrés Escobar takes a moment to sort things out in his hectic world.* David Jacobs / Action Images

time Milla failed to explode until the game that had ended goal–less had progressed into extra time.

Against a fluid Colombian team which, after the elimination of Brazil, played the purest, most classical of South American touch soccer, Cameroon imposed its habitual virtues — a game based on tenacious resistance by a five–man defense, light marking, competent one–touch play and a physical vigor that once again provoked a high ratio of fouls and four yellow cards that would strip it of Emile M'Bouh, André Kana Biyik, Victor N'Dip and Jules Onana for the following game.

Francisco Maturana's Colombian team effectively operated its zonal defense system using Higuita as sweeper and building its offensive moves patiently with neat triangles of short passes, until the rigor of the Cameroon style upset its rhythm.

The stalemate between two contrasting styles lasted until the 16th minute of the extra half–hour. Then Cameroon forward François Omam Biyik sent a through pass to his partner Milla. Milla beat Colombian defender Luis Perea and then dismissed Higuita with a rising left–foot shot.

Two minutes later, Higuita's overconfidence presented Milla with his fourth goal of the tournament, and even though an excellent pass from Carlos Valderamma allowed substitute Bernardo Redín to reduce the margin eight minutes before the final whistle, the Indomitable Lions held out to become the first African nation ever to reach the quarterfinals of the World Cup.

Graham Turner

PERSISTENCE PAYS OFF

YUGOSLAVIA 2 SPAIN 1 (aet). Score at 90 min. 1–1.
Verona. June 26

"Adios. Out Like Brazil!" announced the headlines in Madrid. Spain certainly followed the Brazilian formula of dominating the proceedings, producing its best performance of the tournament, but losing and heading home. The slack pace of the game between two European hopefuls was dictated by an afternoon temperature of 89 degrees in Verona's Nuovo Bentegodi Stadium. Only two players gave the impression of trying to raise the pace. The first was Yugoslavia's creative genius Dragan Stojković, who made full use of Spanish coach Luis Suárez's decision not to field an orthodox left–back to exploit wide open spaces on the right flank. The other was Spanish midfielder Francisco Villaroya, the player attempting manfully to mark Stojković.

By contrast, Spain's potential matchwinner, Emilio Butragueño, was being ably shackled by Refik Sabanadžović. The main danger, however, stemmed from Butragueño's Real Madrid teammates Rafael

Martín Vázquez and Míchel (Miguel González), the skill-ful midfielders.

Just as the Brazilians had done against Argentina, Spain wasted no time in demonstrating that it was bet-ter at moving the ball into danger areas and creating scoring chances, whereas much of the Yugoslav art-istry was restricted to horizontal exercises in the mid-dle of the field.

Spain's Julio Salinas wasted the first clear chance as early as the fourth minute; Butragueño managed to blast a rebound wide of an open goal in the ninth minute after Tomislav Ivković could only partially block a shot from Martín Vázquez. And Martín Vázquez cre-ated three excellent chances for himself with forward dribbling into the Yugoslav penalty area, but on all three occasions he unaccountably opted to aim tamely wide of the near post when teammates were in line at the far post to turn in the cross.

Ivković made a fine save from an Alberto Górriz header in the second half. Butragueño's wretched World Cup was summed up in the 63rd minute when he lost his marker and leapt strongly to connect per-fectly with a Villaroya cross, only to see his header bounce against a post and straight into the arms of a startled and grateful Ivković, who hadn't even moved. Like the Brazilians, the Spaniards could claim they had everything but the killer instinct and luck.

Even the scoring timetable initially followed Brazil-ian guidelines. Extra time was only 12 minutes away when Stojković took a pass from Srećko Katanec, cut the ball inside Martín Vázquez, and beat goalie Andoni Zubizarreta from close in.

Spain scored the tying goal six minutes from the end when Martín Vázquez belatedly decided to aim a shot at the far post for a marauding Salinas to push the ball into an unguarded net.

Barely two minutes of extra time had elapsed when Spain's renewed hopes were again dashed by Stojković on a penalty kick. The speedy Dejan Savićević was fouled by Roberto (Roberto Fernández Bonillo) near the Spanish penalty area. Stojković stepped up and struck a superb free kick over the defensive wall and past Zubizarreta. By this time the heat had taken its toll and Spain's forces were too spent to rally. A Marin Rafa Paz header was the only token gesture in twenty–eight minutes of slow, agonizing death.

The Spaniards, like the Brazilians, were left to la-ment their ill luck in a game well within their reach. Yugoslavia, with "Pixie" Stojković (the nickname stems from his love of "Pixie & Dixie" cartoons, Yugoslavia's version of "Tom & Jerry") playing the role of Maradona, moved on to the quarterfinals. ∎

Graham Turner

ABOVE / *Ivo Knoflíček of Czechoslovakia (left) and Mauricio Montero of Costa Rica battle mano-a-mano for this loose ball.* Alain Landrain / Press•sports

OPPOSITE / *Czech captain Ivan Hašek (right) comes to the aid of goalkeeper Jan Stejskal by gently reminding Costa Rica's Roger Flores of the rules of the house: a 3 of a kind can't beat a full goalie.* Alain Landrain / Press•sports

THE DROUGHT CONTINUES

I n Italy, Spain was looking to cross the threshold from participant to protagonist. Present at every World Cup since 1978, Spain's hopes have always been scuttled by one off–performance or tough break. While Spanish clubs have always been a force in Europe, it has been nearly two decades since the national team of Spain has netted a major success. This year proved no different.

Coach Luis Suárez returned to Italy, where he starred as a player in the sixties, and brought with him a solid team. In the qualifying rounds, Spain had lost only one game (to Austria) and did not allow a single goal at home.

The spine of the team was based on a group of Real Madrid players — Manuel Sanchís, Rafael Martín Vázquez, the skillful midfielder Míchel (Miguel González) and Emilio Butragueño — who had come up through the ranks together and were thought ready to make a mark in Italy.

Spain relied on the scoring of Butragueño, known as "El Buitre" — the Vulture. The fair-haired 27-year-old lurks dangerously around the goalmouth much to the distress of his wary opponents. Butragueño holds the distinction of being the last player to score four goals in a World Cup game (against Denmark in '86). The Vulture's scavenging instincts, however, were off in Italy.

Instead, it was Martín Vázquez who emerged as the team's biggest star. Signed by the Italian team Torino in a multi–million dollar transfer before the World Cup, Martín Vázquez is recognized as a tireless player who does it all.

Spain got away with a tie against Uruguay. Míchel felled South Korea with three outstanding goals, and they won the group by besting Belgium. Against Yugoslavia, Spain sputtered then sparked, only to be extinguished by Dragan Stojković and his two flashes of skillful invention. ■

Keyvan Antonio Heydari

LEFT/ *Julio Salinas of Spain (No. 19) has a golden opportunity to beat Belgian goalie Michel Preud'homme. Though he failed to convert here, Salinas' team beat Belgium, 2-1. After outscoring their qualifying opponents, 20-3, the explosive Spaniards were considered a darkhorse for the World Cup title. A narrow second-round loss to Yugoslavia in extra time ended the dream.* Jon Van Woerden

REFUGE FOR ARTISTS

ork on improving the access roads to the Bentegodi Stadium ran head–first into Verona's cultural heritage. Earthmoving equipment shuddered to a halt against solid Roman walls, roads and tombs, leaving construction companies to butt their heads against brick wall opposition from archaeologists and historians.

Such feuding has been the keynote of Verona's turbulent past, with the shockwaves of epic family quarrels reaching far enough north for William Shakespeare to use a Veronese tragedy as the inspirational backdrop for "Romeo and Juliet".

Mozart, Wagner and Goethe also turned to the city for inspiration and Dante took refuge there when he was expelled from Florence.

There's nothing infernal, however, about the elegant city whose population now nudges the quarter–million mark. Founded on a loop of the River Adige, Verona gained historical importance as one of the prime crossroads in European trading routes and the launching point for access to Austria via the Brenner Pass.

Verona these days is regarded as one of the most complete of northern Italian cities, offering a wealth of monuments belonging to the Roman, Medieval and Renaissance eras. Dominating the famous Piazza Bra is the Arena, dating from the first century A.D. and the second–largest surviving Roman amphitheater after Rome's Colosseum. The Arena, having staged gladiatorial contests, medieval jousting and 17th century theater, has developed, since 1913, into one of the world's most renowned operatic theaters.

Across the Ponte Pietra (the Roman bridge built in the first century B.C. and restored after World War II) the remains of the Roman theater overlooking the river are so evocative of a distant past that visits to 'modern' monuments such as Juliet's famous balcony and her tomb seem almost out of place. ◼

Graham Turner

RIGHT / *Verona is the setting for two of William Shakespeare's plays — Romeo and Juliet and Two Gentlemen of Verona — and provided the stage for four World Cup matches. Hosting plays and playing hosts seem to be roles well suited to this north-central Italian city.* Lehtikuva Oy.

Verona

quarterfinals

DEFENSE DOMINATES

Correctly naming the eight quarterfinalists would have given a clairvoyant a tough time. Few would have dared to discard the Soviets quite so prematurely. Even fewer would have forecast the absence of the European champion, the Netherlands, and the South American champion, Brazil. And fewer still would have put money on the presence of two teams from the British league.

"People have been saying how antiquated, prehistoric and obsolete our playing style is," said English defender Terry Butcher with a sardonic grin, "but here we are with two teams still in. I regard that as a homage to English league football."

However, in terms of crowd-pleasing, the survivors in Italy compare unfavorably with the lineup in Mexico four years previously of France, Brazil, Mexico, West Germany, Spain, Belgium, England and Argentina.

It was at this stage that the abiding impression of mediocrity began to gnaw at the soul. The quarterfinals got by on emotion, patriotism and sympathy for underdogs like Cameroon. But they lacked the ingredients needed to enthrall a worldwide audience of soccer lovers. The statistics tell the story. The four quarterfinals produced seven goals at a dismal average of 1.75 per game. The global average over 60 years of World Cup history was 3.15. The average in Mexico, the poorest-ever, had been almost 50 percent better. Five of the seven goals came in the best match — England and Cameroon. Three of them were penalties. West Germany's solitary goal against the Czechs was also a penalty. And the only other goal scored was the rebound off Irish goalie Patrick Bonner, rammed home by the Italian superman Salvatore "Totò" Schillaci.

Even the heroes had come from unexpected quarters. Schillaci had been a second-division unknown a year previously. England's revelations Paul Gascoigne and David Platt had played minimal roles in the qualifying phase. Top scorer Tomas Skuhravý was a new name to fans outside Czechoslovakia. And the Irish were proving that survival was down to collective endeavor rather than individual virtuosity.

The breakdown of the last eight survivors reveals the split between the nations that were taking the field with the intention of winning, and those that started each game with the intention of not being beaten. Brazil, which had tried to win, had been beaten by an Argentine team obsessed from start to finish with not being beaten and relying on the genius of Diego Maradona to carry the day. Cameroon received an enormous sympathy vote as an outsider, but its priorities were also defensive — at least until Roger Milla could safely be brought into operation. And the supreme example was the Irish team that had reached the quarterfinals without winning a game. It had not been beaten either. Jack Charlton's men had learned to accept their own limitations, play to their strengths and, as top priority, make life impossible for their opponents. The general run of this World Cup was demonstrating that the spoilers were as effective as the creators.

Even England, traditionally associated with an attacking vocation, had reached the quarterfinals with merely a passing mark. Like the Irish, the English were unbeaten and had achieved their modest level of success by adding sweeper Mark Wright as a fifth defender and ordering wingers John

ABOVE / *David Platt and Gary Lineker manage weary smiles after England squeezed out a come-from-behind 3-2 quarterfinal victory, in extra time, over the ever-Indomitable Lions of Cameroon. The English duo accounted for all of their team's goals, two from penalty kicks in the rugged contest.* David Jacobs / Action Images

OPPOSITE / *Though Ivo Knoflíček (No. 17) succeeds here, his Czech teammates just couldn't hold back Guido Buchwald and West Germany for 90 minutes. The Czechs lost the quarterfinal, 1-0, in a match dominated by the Germans more than the score indicates.* Steve Hale / Action Images

THE LIONS ROARED

N o stranger to surprise, Cameroon shocked the 1982 World Cup field by tying all three of its matches and failing to advance only on a goal difference. The 1990 team alleviated that injustice with a scintillating display of style and aggression.

Cameroon excelled despite turmoil behind the scenes. At a pre–tournament training camp in Yugoslavia, goalkeeper Joseph–Antoine Bell lost his starting spot to Thomas N'Kono — one of the 1982 stars — for criticizing the team's preparation and the tactics of Soviet coach Valeri Nepomniatchi.

Cameroon succeeded despite an interesting problem — Nepomniatchi speaks only Russian, which none of his players understand. He apparently was able to get his points across, however, as Cameroon became the first African nation to advance past the first round and into the quarterfinals of a World Cup.

Forward Roger Milla was recalled for the Yugoslavian camp despite his retirement from international play in 1988. All four of his goals were scored as a substitute; two in the second half against Romania, and two more in the second half of overtime against Colombia. So grateful were his countrymen that the capital city of Yaoundé took up a collection to build a statue of him. He starred again in the thrilling quarterfinal against England, coming in after the hour–mark. Milla broke through and was fouled for a penalty kick that Emmanuel Kunde converted to tie the score, 1–1. Four minutes later, he slipped a pass to Eugene Ekéké, who chipped it in for Cameroon's second goal.

Eventually, its defensive lapses conceded two penalty kicks that Gary Lineker converted to eliminate Cameroon. Yet its success netted Africa a third spot in future World Cup tournaments and signaled another striking example of how narrow is the gap between blooming nations and traditional powers. ■

Ridge Mahoney

LEFT / *Somehow, Cameroon's François Omam Biyik did not score over Peter Shilton. Though missing four players disciplined for the team's patented physical play, Cameroon came about this close to upending England. Still, it wasn't a bad run for the Indomitable Lions: they beat the defending world champs from Argentina, became the first African nation to reach the quarterfinals, captured the hearts of world soccer fans, produced an inspirational new hero in 38-year-old Roger Milla, and returned home to a raucous welcome as conquering heroes.*
David Jacobs / Action Images

ABOVE / *The Czechs and Germans went at it hard in their quarterfinal match, and not everyone was left standing.* Steve Hale / Action Images

OPPOSITE (top) / *Team victories are built upon the dozens of individual little contests that stretch across space and time. Here is a face-off between England's Paul Gascoigne and Cameroon's Jean-Claude Pagal (No. 13). Gascoigne begins to push the ball to his right . . .*

(middle) / *. . . so Pagal drops to a slide tackle to stop him.. .*

(bottom) / *. . . but Gascoigne neatly steps through the tackle and continues upfield. Victory: Gascoigne — on to the next showdown!* David Jacobs / Action Images

Barnes and Chris Waddle — two of the team's outstanding individuals — to perform defensive duties in midfield.

Czech coach Jozef Vengloš had no qualms about declaring his intentions before the quarterfinal clash with West Germany. Even though his team had scored 10 times in four matches and Skuhravý was the leading scorer, Vengloš, who was assistant coach when Czechoslovakia beat West Germany on penalties to take the 1976 European Championships, calmly announced that he was aiming for a similar victory in a penalty shootout. The prime aim, he said, was for his team to avoid being beaten. Ironically, a dubious penalty was to stand between the Czechs and their ultimate aim in what should have been a spectacular battle between the two most prolific teams of the tournament.

Amid such a welter of conservatism, Franz Beckenbauer's German team was winning friends for its offense-minded soccer. The Germans, and almost they alone, were prepared to look for space and exploit it; to look for goals — confident they could outscore the opposition. They had conceded one goal in every game played up to the quarterfinals and the four-man defense often looked suspect. But they were prepared to take risks and genuinely tried to win each game. Midfielder Lothar Matthäus had already emerged as one of the major successes of the tournament, and blonde striker Jürgen Klinsmann had been impressive with his strong running, although Beckenbauer was still insisting that he was too selfish. On the day when both Germanies were celebrating their monetary reunification, the West Germans produced their poorest performance of the tournament against a Czech team that was excessively slow in midfield. Beckenbauer's team ran dangerously out of gas in the last 10 minutes, leading to questions about whether the Germans had peaked too soon.

Yugoslavia, in the meantime, remained an enigma, an inconsistent team difficult to categorize. The squad contained fine individual talents such as midfielders "Pixie" Stojković, the young blonde Robert Prosinečki and the immensely gifted Dejan Savićević. All, however, lacked experience. Coach Ivan Osim had yet to solve his jigsaw puzzle selection, and his 4–4–2 alignment looked light on goalscorers.

The Slavs, who had been outplayed by Spain but had won, were to see the other side of the coin against the cynical Argentines. Despite being obliged to play 89 minutes with 10 men after the dismissal of Diego Maradona's marker Refik Sabanadžović, they outshone the world champions and lost on penalties after three of their players failed from 12 yards. Yet again, the World Cup was destroying hallowed concepts of 'may the best team win.'

To all but their own fanatical supporters, the Argentines were already becoming the villains of the World Cup. Their coach, Carlos Bilardo, was continually claiming that everybody else was imitating his playing system, which may have explained the worrying drop in quality. His approach was negative and miserly, based on thwarting and riling the opposition and then praying that Maradona would produce something from his sleeve, apart from his hand.

All this had left the Italians as strong candidates to charge right into the final. The Irish were, technically, not in the same league and seemed unlikely to score against an Italian defense that had yet to concede a goal. However, Italy wasn't a cinch to score against Ireland, either. The Italians were having offensive problems against everyone and they would once again require the magic of Schillaci in the quarterfinals.

Graham Turner

LIONS FINALLY DE-CLAWED

ENGLAND 3 CAMEROON 2 (aet).
Score at 90 min. 2–2. *Naples. July 1*

Two hours before the kickoff between England and Cameroon in San Paolo Stadium the Cameroon players were taking souvenir photos of each other like tourists on the last day of their vacation. Pressure, what pressure?

Four and a half hours later, the same players were squeezing one final effort out of their legs for a lap of honor, and even the English fans gave them a standing ovation. It was hard to believe the Indomitable Lions were the losers.

They returned to Yaoundé to find 20,000 fans waiting stoically in the rain to give them a heroes' welcome, and a million more lined the streets of the capital as they drove to meet Cameroon president Paul Biya. World Cup 1982 veterans Roger Milla and Tommy N'Kono emerged from the palace as Knight Commanders and the rest of the squad was honored with knighthood. That, in the eyes of the

A NATIONAL REBIRTH

I ts tennis transplants are world famous and many of its hockey players compete in the National Hockey League, but soccer still reigns as the top sport in Czechoslovakia. Of the two million athletes registered with its sports association, nearly one–third are soccer players.

Goalkeeper František Planicka, captain of the 1934 team that lost to Italy in the World Cup final, is a revered figure. In 1962, Czechoslovakia again reached the final, only to be beaten by Brazil.

At Italia '90, the national team missed the first free elections in its country since 1946, which were held just two days prior to Czechoslovakia's 5–1 defeat of the United States. Coach Jozef Vengloš and captain Ivan Hašek dedicated the victory to President Václav Havel and the new government. Czechoslovakia's success lasted until the quarterfinals, where it was eliminated by eventual champ West Germany, 1–0. Its only other loss during the tournament was to host Italy after it had already clinched passage to the second round.

Prior to Communist takeover in 1948, Czechoslovakia ranked among the world's top soccer nations. With the birth of the Czechoslovak republic in 1918, league play began, and full professionalism followed a few years later. That ended in the wake of Communist rule.

Not until the late 1980s did the Czechoslovak soccer federation permit players to compete abroad, but the fall of communism has spurred a rush of offers from foreign clubs. In previous years, perennial Czechoslovak league power Sparta Prague dominated the national team, but eight members of the Italia '90 team were under foreign contracts, and several more players found new homes after the tournament. Forward Tomas Skuhravý finished second in World Cup scoring with five goals and left Sparta to sign a contract with Italian club Genoa. ■

Ridge Mahoney

LEFT / *Czech players hold on for dear life in a tense moment against West Germany. Czechoslovakia showed flashes of offensive brilliance during the tournament — they were the only team beside West Germany to twice score four goals or more in a match. But good defenses could also stop them — Italy and West Germany both shut them out.* Steve Hale / Action Images

Cameroon people, was at least a token recompense for having become the first African nation to reach the quarterfinals of the World Cup and, against England, Cameroon came close to advancing to the semifinals.

Even though the program had given the Lions four days more rest than an English team that had struggled for two hours to beat Belgium, Cameroon had been labeled a sacrificial victim after disciplinary bans had stripped them of three defenders and a midfielder. David Platt, finally earning himself a place on the English starting grid, gave England a 1–0 lead when he headed in a pinpoint cross from the aggressive Stuart Pearce in the 25th minute.

Once again, though, Cameroon rallied behind its super–sub, Milla. Just past the hour–mark, he burst into the English penalty box and used his craftiness to lure Paul Gascoigne into a col-

lision. Penalty, indicated Edgardo Codesal, the Mexican referee.

Emmanuel Kunde beat Peter Shilton to tie the score. The Lions' fans roared again when Milla broke through the center of the English defense and slipped a pass to Eugene Ekéké, the reserve who had been on the field less than a minute. He coolly chipped the ball past the exasperated Shilton to put Cameroon in front, 2–1.

The English, who thought they had guaranteed defensive security by opting once again for Mark Wright to come in as fifth man and sweeper, hit the panic button, while the jubilant Lions moved the ball sweetly around and hid it from Bobby Robson's desperate men.

An historic Cameroon victory looked inevitable until the Lions' hunting instincts again led them into trouble. Their record for fouls had been the worst of the tournament, bar Argentina, and two untimely fouls on Gary Lineker were ultimately to cost them their place in history. There were only seven minutes left when the England striker was allowed to get into the Cameroon box with the ball under control. The Lions' instinctive response was a trip from behind.

With normal penalty taker John Barnes back in the dressing room, the job was Lineker's. He did not dis-

appoint and his penalty kick goal at 83 minutes would force the game into extra time.

In extra time, Gascoigne atoned for his earlier indiscretion by feeding Lineker an inspired through pass, and Cameroon goalie Tommy N'Kono was called for fouling the England forward with a desperate dive at his feet. Lineker again outwitted the goalie by blasting the penalty through the center to give England the 3–2 victory. Cameroon took all the plaudits, while England took the semifinal berth.

Graham Turner

WEST GERMANS MOTOR ALONG

WEST GERMANY 1, CZECHOSLOVAKIA 0.
Milan, July 1

West Germany began Italia '90 like a Mercedes, moving effortlessly into overdrive and leaving behind all who came its way.

German teams, like German cars, very rarely let you down. Even when they don't function properly, they still do the job, as Czechoslovakia found out.

Milan and the imposing Giuseppe Meazza–San Siro Stadium, had been the Germans' base in Milan. Some of the team had felt at home from day one — Lothar Matthäus, Jürgen Klinsmann and Andreas Brehme play for Internazionale, which shares the stadium with AC Milan. Others, such as Thomas Berthold and Rudolf Völler, who play for Roma, had been regular visitors with their clubs.

Germany was favored, it usually is, but Czechoslovakia arrived with the competition's leading goalscorer, Tomas Skuhravý, and his speed partner in goals Ivo Knoflíček.

The Czech strikers, however, rarely saw the ball. Their teammates were too busy trying to contain a rampant German team that dominated possession and virtually every other facet of the game.

Czechoslovakia created little because it was penned back in its own half for long periods, having to adopt to a siege mentality against opponents who attacked everywhere.

The turning point of the game came in the 24th minute when Klinsmann collected a pass on the left. He dribbled past two defenders into the penalty area. As Jozef Chovanec and František Straka moved in to challenge, Klinsmann went down.

Referee Helmut Kohl immediately pointed to the penalty spot.

Matthäus took the penalty kick. As goalie Jan Stejskal dove to his right, the ball sped past on the other side. It was the fourth goal of Italia '90 for the German captain and was to be the only one of this quarterfinal match.

ABOVE / *Cameroon erupts in a triple-decker celebration after scoring a goal against England. Team captain Stephen Tataw holds his head in disbelief, while Bertin Ebwelle enjoys the ride upstairs.* David Jacobs / Action Images

Milano

SOCCER CAPITAL OF THE WORLD

When Italy played Austria in the semifinals of the World Cup on June 3, 1934, tickets cost just a few cents. Despite Italy's victory, the headlines in the newspapers the following morning were about Luigi Pirandelo's Nobel Prize for literature.

Fifty–six years later, soccer dominated Milan's newspaper headlines and tickets to the tournament opener, hosted by Milan, cost up to $150. Scalpers charged five times that amount.

Milan, a leader in business, media and fashion, still likes to consider it foremost a football city, and if there is an air of arrogance about the Milanese when they talk about soccer, it is understandable.

AC Milan is the European and World Club champions, and it shares the Giuseppe Meazza–San Siro Stadium, rated by most as the world's finest soccer stadium, with rival club Inter Milan.

In a sport ruled by a "how much?" mentality, AC Milan has benefited from the deep pockets of its TV magnate owner and stocked the field with top–flight players, including the Dutch threesome, Frank Rijkaard, Ruud Gullit and Marco van Basten. (So prevalent is the trend to buy and trade world–class players, Italy allows only three foreigners to play at a time to keep a balance among the teams.)

While Milan ceded to Napoli then Inter in the two previous seasons of the Italian league, it has led the major European competitions for the past two years.

Inter has yet to surpass its record–setting '88–89 season in the Italian league when it took the championship, but it could take satisfaction in the fact that three of its regular season players — Lothar Matthäus, Jürgen Klinsmann and Andreas Brehme — were on the winning team.

Christopher Davies

LEFT / *Milan's Galleria is a world–class gathering place for tourists and the Milanese alike.* Massimo Siragusa / AC

OPPOSITE / *Though Milan seems the typical Italian city in the silhouette of its Piazza del Duomo, it proclaims itself as something more: the soccer capital of the world. This bold declaration is backed by the city's two successful club teams, which employ many of the world's best players. Indeed, Milan hosted six World Cup games, as many as Rome.* David Jacobs / Action Images

LEFT / *Maybe our eyes are playing tricks, but it seems that Fernando De Napoli of Italy is about to receive a good, swift kick from Ireland's Niall Quinn . . .*

BELOW / *. . . but De Napoli bounces up to make a determined rush upfield, leaving behind a puzzled Quinn.* David Jacobs / Action Images

OPPOSITE / *Ireland wasn't the only team handing out quarterfinal punishment — Italy's Paolo Maldini gets in a stout forearm cross.* David Jacobs / Action Images

ABOVE / *After a hard-fought battle against Ireland, victory was especially sweet for the Italians, whose 1-0 win secured a place in the semifinals.* David Jacobs / Action Images

IRISH EYES
ARE SMILIN'

T he Republic of Ireland failed to win a game in Italia '90, was involved in probably the two most sterile ties of the tournament, and, in the words of coach Jack Charlton, did not play pretty football — yet returned to a heroes' reception in Dublin.

When Charlton became coach in February 1986, Ireland was an underachiever, never having qualified for a major finals.

Charlton decided not to take on the world at what the world did better, so he devised a system to make the most of the traditional attributes of British football.

The Irish tried to play the game in their opponents' half, not in an area where damage could be done. This generally meant a long, hopeful clearance from defense, often bypassing midfield.

Ireland's players also closed down the opposition with their harrying defense. Pretty? No. Pretty effective? Yes.

The Republic reached the finals of the 1988 European Championships and qualified for the 1990 World Cup. Charlton, the man who helped England win the 1966 World Cup, was made an honorary Irishman. Apart from the Pope, he is the best–loved foreigner in Ireland.

The Irish are the draw specialists of the world and Italia '90 typified Ireland's record — four draws and a 1–0 defeat by Italy.

The games against the Netherlands, Romania (beaten on penalties) and Italy were played with passion showing that Ireland was not quite the ugly duckling it had been labeled.

While the Irish style may not be to everyone's liking, there can be no argument that their supporters are a role model for others. After the Irish succumbed to Italy in the quarterfinals, the Irish fans stood singing and waving flags, enjoying the occasion for half an hour. When, at last, Charlton emerged, the Irish fans gave the honorary Irishman the sort of welcome usually reserved for winners. ■

Christopher Davies

RIGHT / *Fans from Ireland and Italy test their luck-attracting abilities with the help of this Italian lass. Heaven forbid, Irish luck went Italy's way this time. But the team from Eire prospered through a stout defense and plain ol' hard work. Ireland allowed just three goals in five matches, never more than one in a game.*
David Jacobs / Action Images

ABOVE / *There are more than enough legs and arms to go around in this major midfield traffic jam. Let's untangle things here — that's West Germany's Jürgen Kohler (No. 4) and England's Gary Lineker (No. 10).*
David Jacobs / Action Images

semifinals

RUSSIAN ROULETTE

A nd then there were four — Italy, England, Argentina and West Germany. The semifinal match–ups featured the host team — and favorite — Italy against an intriguing Argentina squad led by Diego Maradona and European adversaries England and West Germany, who had met in the 1966 World Cup final in England.

After the 90-minute regular time period, there were still four teams remaining as both games were tied 1-1. And after the extra times, the opponents for the final had still not been decided.

It seemed fitting that in a World Cup dominated by defense and noted for its number of penalty kicks and shootouts that the two contestants to reach the final of the world's premier sporting event would be determined by football's version of Russian Roulette.

Italy, which had not lost a game going into the semifinals, went down 4-3 on penalties to Argentina, the South Americans' second successive shootout victory. Argentina reached its second consecutive final by winning just two games, against the USSR and, with a great deal of good fortune, Brazil.

England suffered exactly the same fate as Italy against West Germany, also falling 4-3 on penalty kicks.

West Germany and Italy had played the best soccer throughout the tournament but while coach Franz Beckenbauer's team survived the shootout with England, plucky Argentina's success on penalty kicks prevented what might have been a dream match–up in the final: Italy vs West Germany.

But games are won and lost on the field, not on paper and the Italia '90 semifinals proved that in dramatic fashion.

THE KISS OF DEATH

ARGENTINA 1 ITALY 1 (aet). 4–3 on penalties.
Naples, July 3

Italy was one of the few countries to have lived up to expectations during the World Cup. The Italians had won all their first–round games (though struggling against a spirited U.S. team) and had overcome the varied challenges of Uruguay and the Republic of Ireland.

They were favored to beat Argentina, which had reached the semifinals with considerable good fortune and by converting more penalties than its opponents.

ABOVE / *West Germany's Andreas Brehme and teammates gleefully sprint down the field after Brehme's goal gave his team a 1-0 lead over England in the entertaining semifinal match in Turin.*
David Jacobs / Action Images

Argentina had carried its macho image to the extreme: It arrived in Naples having collected 15 yellow cards. Eight of its players walked the tightrope of one yellow card and four were cited during the semifinals, thus robbing them of a place in the final.

Argentina had used 20 players with only three, Diego Maradona, Juan Simón and José Basualdo, playing every game.

Italy, yet to concede a goal, had kept its defense unchanged. It found the striker it had been searching for in Salvatore Schillaci, who had netted four of Italy's six goals. Italy's goalscoring problems were perfectly illustrated by the fact that going into the World Cup the highest scorer on the team was right–back Giuseppe Bergomi, who had just six goals to his credit in 71 international appearances.

Schillaci, who placed an extra burden on himself by promising to score before each game, was as good as his word again against Argentina. He gave the hosts the lead in the 17th minute, starting and finishing off the move.

Torino

ABOVE / *Home of automaker Fiat, the Holy Shroud and the peaceful Po River, which favorably reflects many of the city's landmarks, Turin was a proud host of Brazil's four matches and the semifinal between West Germany and England.* Paolo Siccardi / AC

STRATEGIC TOWNSHIP REJUVENATED

ABOVE / *Though Turin is Italy's fourth largest city, it is not usually thought of as a tourist haven in the same way as Rome, Venice, Naples or Florence. But who can argue with the beauty of this twilight tableau in Italy's Alps-shadowed northwestern metropolis?* Paolo Siccardi / AC

Turin is probably most recognized for its turn–of–the–century association with the Fiat automobile company. The company employs — directly or indirectly — 70 percent of the workers among the million plus population.

The city, overlooked on three sides by the Alps, straddles the River Po as it flows across the Plains of Padana. As a strategic township on the main route between Rome and continental Europe, this Roman city, named Julia Augusta Taurinorum, was devastated by Hannibal and his elephants as soon as they had crossed the Alps in the third century B.C., and was thereafter regularly sacked by passing barbarians.

In the 10th century, Turin was absorbed by the House of Savoy and embarked on economic expansion under alternating periods of French and Italian domination and, even today, retains a close cultural connection with its French neighbors. Turin played a major part in Italian unification and was the emerging nation's capital between 1861 and 1865.

Inevitably, Turin's soccer bears the Fiat trademark. The Agnelli family, long–term sponsors of Juventus, has recently invested $30 million in new players and coaching staff in a bid to wrest supremacy from Milan. The Stadio delle Alpi, specially built for the World Cup, now takes over from the old Communale as the scene for the passionate local matches between Juventus and Torino.

Graham Turner

ABOVE (top) / *Italian captain Giuseppe Bergomi (foreground) uses his considerable wingspan to block out hot-pursuing Claudio Caniggia . . .*

(bottom) / *. . . causing the Argentine star to momentarily retreat. Though he lost the battle here, Caniggia and his teammates won the war, claiming a hard-earned victory over the home team.* David Jacobs / Action Images

The Juventus striker followed up when Argentine goalie Sergio Goycochea could only block Gianluca Vialli's shot. Schillaci looked like he may have been offside, but the flag stayed down.

Walter Zenga, Italy's goalkeeper, achieved a personal milestone in the 52nd minute when he beat the record by England's Peter Shilton of 499 minutes in the World Cup without conceding a goal. In his previous 19 international appearances, Zenga had conceded only three goals. His record was to stay intact for only another 16 minutes because in the 68th minute Argentina scored.

Zenga must shoulder much of the blame. He went after but failed to reach Julio Olarticoechea's tempting pass. Claudio Caniggia beat both Zenga and Riccardo Ferri to flick the ball into the empty net.

Since the arrival of Maradona in Naples, the locals have been used to celebrating goals by Argentines but the San Paolo stadium was stunned.

Italy was in control of the game, but slowly but surely a combination of Maradona's prompting and never–say–die spirit brought Argentina back.

There were to be no more goals in regular time. The reigning World Champions had clawed their way back against the team expected to become World Champions. There was heartbreak as well as joy for Argentina in the next 30 minutes.

Extra time was as unpleasant as the first 90 minutes had been pleasing. Like the best athletes who peak when it really matters, Argentina had played its best football of the tournament. It was becoming apparent that Italy did not have the temperament to handle the pressure.

In the 112th minute Argentina's Ricardo Giusti was shown the red card for an off–the–ball incident involving Roberto Baggio, who was left holding his jaw. Argentina was furious. Players and coaches surrounded French referee Michel Vautrot and Danish linesman Peter Mikkelsen who had spotted the offense.

One's memory went back to Argentina vs England at Wembley in 1966 when Rattin refused to leave Wembley. Such was the delay before Giusti went that the first half of extra time lasted 23 minutes and 21 seconds instead of 15 minutes.

Argentina's 10 men held out against Italy's 11. Having beaten Yugoslavia on penalties in the third round in Florence, the World Champions once again had to do so to retain a chance to defend their title.

The first six penalties were successful. Then up stepped Roberto Donadoni, ironically one of Italy's best players of the tournament. Goycochea dove to his left and saved the penalty — now Maradona, who had missed against Yugoslavia, would have to drive the nail in the coffin of his adopted country.

His nerve did not fail him, and when Goycochea saved Aldo Serena's shot, Argentina celebrated its

TOP / *There's nothing tongue-in-cheek about the way Argentina's Diego Maradona aggressively advances the ball, or how the superstar is watched like a hawk by three (count 'em!) Italian defenders.* David Jacobs / Action Images

ABOVE / *With their backs consistently against the wall, Diego Maradona (No. 10), Ricardo Giusti (No. 14), Jorge Burruchaga (No. 7) and their Argentine teammates pulled together when they needed to — almost to the very end.* David Jacobs / Action Images

RIGHT / *Italy's Salvatore Schillaci promised a goal against Argentina, then doggedly worked to back up his brash words. He was in the right place at the right time and struck the nets only 17 minutes into the semifinal — his sixth score of the tournament, and his last.* David Jacobs / Action Images

BOBBY'S BOYS

In the months leading up to the World Cup, England coach Bobby Robson had to endure criticism that bordered on the hysterical and libelous.

Days before England left for its training camp in Sardinia, Robson announced he was joining PSV Eindhoven of Holland after the World Cup "because I didn't think there was a job for me here."

The tabloids had to do an abrupt about-turn after England's success, however unexpected it may have been. The man called a "Plonker" became a hero. The newspaper that urged "Bring 'Em All Home Now" after the opening 1-1 draw against Ireland was searching for superlatives to heap upon Bobby's Boys.

England started Italia '90 slowly but improved steadily, accepting luck as it came its way.

It lost to West Germany on penalties in the semifinals but won the respect of the world. Paul Gascoigne, criticized for his inconsistency, was England's finest attacking player. Des Walker was as good a defender as there was on view at World Cup '90.

Peter Shilton, the world's most "capped" player in his 41st year, showed that the sands of time had not affected his reflexes.

England, winner in 1966, had never reached the final four on foreign soil. Italia '90, therefore, was an historic achievement, the perfect way for Robson to bow out.

Combining traditional virtues like fitness, durability, heart and character with skill, England deserved its success. ■

Christopher Davies

OPPOSITE / *This shot, redirected only a few inches, might have sent England to the World Cup Final. West German goalie Bodo Illgner makes a spectacular save as Gary Lineker watches. Lineker later scored, but the English lost on penalties. This was a team wrapped in turmoil, but one that eventually pleased even its demanding fans and media.* David Jacobs / Action Images

ABOVE / *One of the reasons for England's fine showing was 40-year-old goalkeeper Peter Shilton, whose play receives the stamp of approval from West German coach Franz Beckenbauer moments after the Germans' razor-thin victory.* David Jacobs / Action Images

THE GOOD,
THE BAD,
THE BEAUTIFUL

T his bustling port city lies in the crescent of Campania, a quarter–moon set in the Bay of Naples. Water so blue as to appear incandescent and sky only slightly less striking lend the city a surrealistic feel that evaporates in streets brimming with kamikaze vehicles and market squares choked with haggling crowds. Mount Vesuvius lies just a few miles to the south, and Neapolitans themselves erupt often.

The latest such occurrence came on April 29, when Diego Maradona led Napoli to its second Italian championship. Napoli, formed in 1926, had never won a title prior to Maradona's arrival in 1986 just weeks after he led Argentina to its second World Cup. Maradona brought Naples it first championship in his first season, triggering celebrations that packed Neapolitan streets with a new form of gridlock. In just one example of Neapolitan madness, fans plastered photos of dead relatives to car windows for the celebrations, with the explanation that papa or grandpa or uncle wouldn't have wanted to miss out on the fun.

Napoli won its second title five weeks before the start of the World Cup, returning Maradona to the throne he'd fallen off at the start of the season by reporting late to training camp and supposedly flirting with a team in France.

All of Italy mourned, though, when Maradona led Argentina to its 1–0 triumph over Italy in the same stadium where he had played for Napoli. A mob of heartbroken fans took it out on Maradona by stoning his villa. But just a few days after the final, Maradona promised to report for training camp on time, and Neapolitans eagerly looked toward the 1990–91 season in which Napoli would not only defend its league title, but also compete in the European Champions' Cup, the ultimate prize for Continental clubs. ■

Ridge Mahoney

OPPOSITE / *Naples has a frenetic pace all its own. Maybe the daily sight of Mt. Vesuvius reminds Neapolitans to squeeze the most from each day. Still, the serene can be found amidst this bedlam, for instance on the city's picturesque harbor . . .*

ABOVE / *. . . or in the intricate work of this craftswoman.* Luca Musella / AC

PAGE 142 / *The sight of referee Edgardo Codesal surrounded by angry and wildly gesticulating Argentine players was a common one.* David Jacobs / Action Images

PAGE 143 / *The victory might not have come in the dramatic and triumphant manner players fantasize about in daydreams, but it was a world championship nonetheless.* David Jacobs / Action Images

Napoli

finals

talia '90 had unfolded as a tournament of unfulfilled hopes and delightful surprises, and its final weekend followed that scenario in matches of stark contrast.

Unfortunately, the final between Argentina and West Germany wore the stigma of disappointment. No fireworks from Diego Maradona; little of the flair West Germany flashed in earlier games; and more frustrating examples of atrocious refereeing at critical points.

In contrast, Italy and England had whirled through a fascinating third–place match the day before. Both teams shook away the crushing disappointment of shootout defeats in the semifinals, and the Italian fans rose out of their black clouds of mourning with a festive display.

Despite their different complexions, the two matches shared some distinguishing features. Both were decided by penalty kicks, both suffered from rotten refereeing, and both said farewell to several bright stars.

The 1990 final was a rematch of the 1986 final which Argentina won, 3–2. This final was to be much less satisfying. Argentina, without four players because of suspensions and with a Maradona hobbled by injuries, petulantly throttled the match. Coach Carlos Bilardo imposed a straightjacket scheme by packing the defensive third of the field.

Argentina had played superb soccer in 1986, which made its stagnant showing in 1990 all the more aggravating. No matter. Buenos Aires celebrated as if Argentina had repeated its '86 triumph, and President Carlos Menem again hosted team members at the stately Pink House, where the FIFA trophy had been displayed for the past four years.

Beckenbauer, who'd announced before the tournament he was stepping down from the national team post, left as the only man to captain (1974) and coach a World Cup champion. West Germany played in an unprecedented third straight final and joined Brazil and Italy as three–time World Cup champions.

USED
TO
INVASIONS

Nestled next to the Adriatic Sea on the east coast of Italy, Bari's history is one of turbulence. It's been invaded by Normans, Greeks, Arabs, Romans, and Spaniards, among others, and the results can be seen in its diverse architecture. Its most modern structure is the Nuovo Stadio Comunale, built for the 1990 World Cup. The old stadium was home for club team Bari, and hosted just four internationals, one of which was the debut of Italian sweeper Franco Baresi in 1983.

Had World Cup organizers known what surprises were to be sprung in Group B, they might have pondered reworking the draw. The first game in Bari produced Romania's sporting and political shocker, a 2–0 upset of the Soviet Union. The Soviets never recovered from the defeat and crashed out of the tournament in the first round.

A week after that match, however, came the modern version of past insurgencies. Journalists invaded Bari — a privileged few by plane, most by arduous train trips of at least nine hours — in pursuit of tournament darlings Cameroon. After dumping Argentina in the World Cup opener in Milan, the effervescent Cameroonians had swept past Romania 2–1 and become Africa's first qualifier for the second round of a World Cup. For a few days at least, 38–year–old wonder Roger Milla and his teammates owned the city — not the first time foreigners have ruled.

Local team Bari has never won an Italian title in its 82 years of operation and, in fact, has spent most of that time in the second division. But it won promotion last spring, and among the additions for Serie A competition is Romanian forward Florin Raducioiu. The move in some ways closed an ancient circle; most of Romania was the Roman province of Dacia from 100 to 271 A.D. ■

Ridge Mahoney

ABOVE / *Bari, like many other Italian cities, has a charming way of juxtaposing the new with the old (or even ancient). Here, this year's blooms adorn the hillside below the unique, 750-year-old Castel del Monte outside of the city.* courtesy of ENIT-NY

OPPOSITE / *Nestled in relative obscurity on the southeastern Italian coast, Bari has not enjoyed many of its visitors in the past — they came as invaders. But this charming city threw open its arms for 1990's invasion of soccer players and aficionados and was rewarded with some of the tournament's most interesting games, including Italy's third-place victory over England.* courtesy of ENIT-SF

Bari

Argentina's Nestor Lorenzo (No. 13) finds an uncooperative dance partner in Jürgen Klinsmann of West Germany. The outmanned Argentines, missing four of their players due to suspension and losing two more to expulsion during the final, slowed the pace — Germany wanted to jitterbug; Argentina chose to waltz.

David Jacobs / Action Images

Franz Beckenbauer surveys his realm and its subjects before the big match. This was to be his night, the night he would become the first person to win World Cup titles as both captain and coach . . .

. . . but Argentina slowed down the game and gummed up the German scoring machine by collapsing into a tight defensive bundle . . .

. . . and though the Germans peppered Argentine goalie Sergio Goycochea with shots and had many golden scoring opportunities, their frustration grew as none made their way into the net . . .

. . . and Argentina, though obviously outmanned, continued to doggedly pursue each loose ball as the clock wound down toward a scoreless tie. Would the "Hand of God" again come to the rescue of Argentina? . . .

. . . It almost did. Andreas Brehme's penalty kick in the 84th minute beat Goycochea, hit the post . . . and skittered into the net. The pendulum that had for so long moved Argentina's way swooped back with one dramatic swing. The title was West Germany's — and Beckenbauer's. David Jacobs / Action Images

ABOVE / *Italians, though stunned by the semifinal loss to Argentina, still relished the chance to see Totò —Salvatore Schillaci — fearlessly charge upfield one more time in the match for third place. Schillaci, and his team, didn't disappoint, beating England, 2-1.*
David Jacobs / Action Images

RIGHT / *Confusion abounds — Italy's Ciro Ferrara (No. 5), England's David Platt and a gaggle of others can't quite seem to decide what to do with this loose ball.*
David Jacobs / Action Images

But this was a more skilled, more explosive team than the 1982 and 1986 squads that had started slowly and survived more by grit than grace. West Germany roared through the first round with 10 goals in three games, then seemed to flatten out after knocking out the Netherlands, 2–1, in a classic second–round showdown. In the end, its zealous commitment to fitness and resilient spirit carried it to victory, even though it was unable to play better as the competition got tougher.

"If we had played Italy," said Beckenbauer, "the world would have seen a much more vibrant, exciting match. Argentina was so negative. It was just defense."

THE HOST TEAM RECOVERS

Italy 2, England 1 Bari, July 7

Italy had thrived on defense and the opportunistic strikes of Salvatore "Totò" Schillaci up to the semifinals, but its suspect composure finally cracked against Argentina. National pride returned in Italy's 2–1 victory over a courageous English team.

England coach Bobby Robson, in his last hurrah before taking over at Dutch club PSV Eindhoven, brought in Tony Dorigo for his first World Cup match and gave a starting spot to Trevor Steven, an invaluable substitute during the tournament. Italian coach Azeglio Vicini used Ciro Ferrara and Pietro Vierchowod in defense, and gave old warhorse Carlo Ancelotti his final run in midfield.

England lacked midfield virtuoso Paul Gascoigne because of suspension, yet again displayed the skillful flourishes that had nearly undone West Germany. The Italians could not dominate midfield as they had against most of their opponents, but attacked vigorously. A match brimming with enthusiasm and sportsmanship resulted — no red or yellow cards, plenty of intelligent passes, clean tackles, and good scoring opportunities.

Italy found its greatest success through the middle of England's defense, the area Cameroon had repeatedly pierced. Roberto Baggio tested English goalie Peter Shilton more than once, and Schillaci lurked darkly in the goalmouth like a badger ready to pounce. He could have scored in the 17th minute when Peter Shilton brilliantly tipped a shot by Ferrara onto the post, but the rebound escaped him.

England played effective balls to the flanks, and was unlucky not to take the lead when Gary Lineker's header beat goalie Walter Zenga but hit one of his defenders in the back.

Still, neither team could score until the most experienced player in the history of the game committed a rookie mistake. Shilton, to the left of his net, leisurely

ABOVE / *English goalie Peter Shilton doesn't look his age — 40 — nor did he play his age throughout a brilliant tournament.* David Jacobs / Action Images

pursued a rolling ball near the goal line. A warning shout alerted him; he looked over his right shoulder and saw Baggio knifing in for the steal. The goalie lowered his shoulder and clobbered Baggio to the ground, but not before he'd tapped the ball free.

Ferrara controlled the loose ball on the wing as a panicked English defense tried to reset. Baggio waved for a penalty from a prone position, then got up and was a yard offside when Ferrara returned the ball to him. No flag, no whistle, so Baggio slinked through defenders to blast a point–blank shot high into the net.

Robson immediately sent on midfielder Chris Waddle and Neil Webb, and after the latter forced Zenga to make a fine, diving save of his low shot, England tied the match with 10 minutes remaining. Dorigo got free on the left wing and had more than enough time to swerve across. David Platt leaped and nailed an unstoppable header past Zenga.

A fourth straight extra–time session seemed likely, but referee Joel Quiniou awarded Italy a penalty kick with six minutes left. Schillaci had chased a ball into the box and had appeared to lose possession when he bundled into defender Paul Parker and fell. But he was given the penalty and stroked it past Shilton for the winner.

In the final seconds, Nicola Berti ran onto a long flighted ball and stabbed a header into the net. Unbelievably, linesman Mohammed Hansal flagged for offside, and even more unbelievably, Quiniou disallowed the goal. Berti had been five yards onside when the ball was kicked. This was simply the most glaring example of abysmal offside decisions that plagued Italia '90. Hansal had failed to flag Baggio offside on Italy's first goal, too.

With six goals, Schillaci took the Golden Shoe award as the tournament's top scorer, and 1986 scoring leader Lineker handed over the baton with a warm embrace after the final whistle.

CALCIO = FOOTBALL

Football in English and French, *futbol* in Spanish, *futebol* in Portuguese, *fussball* in German, *voetbal* in Dutch, *fotoboll* in Swedish, even *futobol* in Turkish ... but *calcio* in Italian. *Calcio*? A linguistic aberration?

Not exactly. It was a certain Luigi Bosisio who, according to the Gazzette delo Sport on October 18, 1907, proposed that Italy create its own word for the sport which was sweeping the country after its introduction by the British. Bosisio suggested an adaptation of the word "to kick" —*calciare* —hence *calcio* (and never mind the fact that the word also means "calcium" and "rifle butt").

Source: WORLD CUP NEWS, Kick-Off Edition, ISL Marketing, Lucerne, Switzerland.

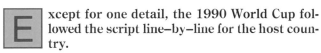

RICH IN CALCIO

Except for one detail, the 1990 World Cup followed the script line–by–line for the host country.

That detail, unfortunately, was reaching the final, a glaring injustice that stripped the tournament of a potentially glorious spectacle: Italy taking on West Germany for the title in the Olympic Stadium, and perhaps repeating its triumph of 1934 — a 2–1 overtime win over Czechoslovakia in the old Falminio Stadium.

Its loss on penalty kicks to Argentina pricked Italy's balloon. Enthusiasm began whooshing out of the tournament almost immediately. Vendors disappeared from the streets of Rome, restaurants and shops reverted to their traditional closing hours of Saturday afternoon and all day on Sunday.

Yet Italy justified its prestige as soccer's "Center Court." In the Argentina–West Germany final, no less than 13 of the 22 starters were under contract to Italian club teams. Every tournament match featured Italian jerseys, scarves, banners and flags, vivid icons of the country's passion for *calcio*.

Italians have a tremendous zeal for the nation's unofficial religion. After all, the Pope had been a goalie in his youth, a heritage most Italians not just share, but revel in all their lives.

Italy's stature as the richest soccer nation produced an unprecedented sweep in all three European club tournaments. AC Milan took the Champions' Cup, Sampdoria captured the Cup–Winners' Cup, and Juventus won the UEFA Cup. That portended well for the World Cup, but Argentina — where soccer took root largely because of Italian immigrants — denied the hosts their ultimate goal. ■

Ridge Mahoney

LEFT / *So this is the stuff that turned Salvatore Schillaci into a sudden superman for the World Cup. We're sure the Gatorade marketing people have taken due notice.* David Jacobs / Action Images

Roma

ETERNAL PLAYGROUND

Just as Rome once controlled the largest empire in world history, the world's greatest sporting event centered itself on the Eternal City. A vast press center went up just outside the Stadio Olimpico, and journalists from around the world sunned themselves next to the Olympic pool.

Nearly 2,000 years before Italia '90, Romans erected monuments to sporting competition. Dedicated in 80 A.D., the Colosseum is the most famous and largest and said to have accommodated 50,000 spectators. The Forum and Circus Maximus once echoed to thundering hooves during chariot races.

Romans also played ball games and spread them around Europe. Not all involved kicking the ball; "harpastrum" permitted use of both arms and feet. These games were primitive forerunners to the games the British exported throughout their own empire more than a millennia later, and eventually evolved into soccer, rugby, American football, etc.

Dictator Benito Mussolini used soccer and war to build national enthusiasm for his Fascist doctrines. Italy hosted and won the 1934 World Cup, playing all its matches but one at the old Stadio Flaminio in Rome. Renovations at the Olympic Stadium, built in 1953, forced Italian club teams Lazio and Roma to use Flaminio during the league season.

Italy's five victories in the Olympic Stadium during Italia '90 kept its World Cup record in Rome perfect: eight wins, no losses. ∎

Ridge Mahoney

LEFT / *These Roman columns have watched the tides of history through generations, back to the time when Rome ruled the world. For one happy month, Rome again ruled the world — of soccer.*
Cynthia Greer

THE THIRD TIME'S A CHARM

Although lovers of Brazilian magic may protest, West Germany took over the mantle of the most successful country in World Cup competition at Italia '90.

Losers in the 1982 and 1986 finals with relatively undistinguished teams, the West Germans this time featured several of the world's top players. Coach Franz Beckenbauer assembled a formidable team built around five stars playing for Italian clubs. Despite tailing off after the second round, West Germany battled past Czechoslovakia and survived a penalty-kick showdown to eliminate old rival England, thus becoming the only team to play in three straight World Cup finals.

By beating Argentina, 1–0, West Germany joined Italy and Brazil as three–time world champions. It won the 1954 final against Hungary, the only defeat that nation suffered in six years of international play. As host in 1974, West Germany, captained by Beckenbauer, toppled the great Dutch team of Johan Cruyff in the final by a 2–1 score in Munich. In the second round of Italia '90, the West Germans again beat the Dutch by the same score in a tense, exciting battle that ranked as one of the tournament's best matches.

The West Germans scored the most goals in the tournament (15), with captain Lothar Matthäus netting four and defender Andy Brehme and striker Jürgen Klinsmann each getting three.

A tie with Colombia was the only match West Germany didn't win. Its World Cup record of 38 wins, 14 losses and 10 ties doesn't match Brazil's 48–12–13, but no country comes close to its incredible mark of six finals and eight semifinals in 10 appearances since World War II. ∎

Ridge Mahoney

LEFT / *In the end, there was no holding back Guido Buchwald and West Germany. The Germans had too much depth, too many weapons, and too rich a tradition behind it. West Germany won its third world title, matching Italy and Brazil. It has reached the final game an astounding six times in its 10 tournament appearances since World War II. There was little doubt that the best team won World Cup 1990.* Daniel Motz / MOTZSPORTS

Despite its flaws, this World Cup tournament still grabbed the world's attention in a big way, much as Argentina's José Serrizuela (No. 18) does to West Germany's Pierre Littbarski here. Rough play, low scoring, a tidal wave of goals by penalty — but it's still a spectacle followed the world over. David Jacobs / Action Images

England, its devotion to fairness admired throughout the competition, won the Fair Play Award for fewest disciplinary violations.

JUSTICE IS SERVED

West Germany 1, Argentina 0

Without his Gang of Four, Bilardo had few options for a starting 11. Claudio Caniggia was out, as were midfielders Julio Olarticochea and Ricardo Giusti, and defender Daniel Batista.

Beckenbauer chose Pierre Littbarski and Thomas Hässler to support Lothar Matthäus in midfield and deployed Guido Buchwald to mark Maradona. Four years before, he'd assigned Matthäus to shadow the great Argentine, and so anemic was West Germany's attack only the late arrival of Karlheinz Rummenigge had sparked it to life.

And, of course, it was Beckenbauer himself assigned to mark England's brilliant Bobby Charlton in the 1966 World Cup final. West Germany's attack suffered, and even though it had scraped an equalizing goal in the final minutes, England eventually won in extra time.

With West Germany's errant finishing, extra time loomed a distinct possibility to conclude Italia '90. Argentina defended by zonally stacking its players, yet West Germany repeatedly turned inviting balls across the goal. Rudi Völler squandered four all by himself and set the tone just two minutes into the game with a close–range miss. That was one of the many shots created by left–back Andreas Brehme, who bombarded the goalmouth with crosses and free kicks Völler couldn't put away and Jürgen Klinsmann couldn't reach.

So thorough was West Germany's domination it outshot Argentina 16–1 during the match, and the South Americans' only attempt came when Maradona curled a free kick well over the crossbar. Without Caniggia to run down balls and stretch the defense with his speed, Argentina had only Gustavo Dezotti up front. Maradona had worked with Dezotti in training prior to the final, showing him how to read the balls Caniggia exploited, but the homework couldn't solve their offensive problems.

At halftime, Bilardo replaced defender Oscar Ruggeri with Pedro Monzón. Nothing, though, could stem the tide of threatening balls dropping in at the far post. Three minutes into the second half, Brehme curled a free kick over the Argentine defense to Thomas Berthold. He tried to head the ball on the bounce, but shot it well over the bar. Two minutes later, same situation and result, except it was Völler whose shot went almost straight up as he stretched his right leg to meet the ball. And so it went, with Klinsmann, too, off the mark.

Bilardo pulled off the ineffective Jorge Burruchaga and replaced him with Gabriel Calderón. The substitu-

ABOVE / *Two of Italy's best offensive weapons — Salvatore Schillaci (No. 19) and Roberto Baggio — embrace in a moment of celebration following a goal against England. The duo accounted for Italy's two scores in the match.* Steve Hale / Action Images

ABOVE / *West Germany's Andreas Brehme stabs the air in jubilation after his penalty kick, though barely, found its mark. Teammates Jürgen Klinsmann (No. 18) and Pierre Littbarski (No. 7) rush in to greet the soaring scorer when he comes back down out of the clouds.*

Jon Van Woerden

tion ended a disastrous tournament for Burruchaga, scorer of the winning goal in the 1986 final. Even luck ran against him; in the quarterfinal against Yugoslavia with three minutes left in overtime, he'd steered in a cross from José Basualdo, but the referee said the ball came off his arm and not his chest.

In the 64th minute, the volatile cauldron boiled over. Klinsmann broke free on the right and was chopped by a hard foul from Monzón. Referee Edgardo Codesal showed him the red card. Some felt the ejection was too harsh, some agreed emphatically. The match had certainly turned rougher in the second half, and perhaps Codesal weighed this increasing violence into his decision.

With six minutes left, Codesal called the crucial penalty. Matthäus had marched through midfield before sliding a diagonal ball into the right–hand side of Argentina's penalty area. Völler angled to control the ball, and defender Roberto Sensini cut in front of him to tackle the ball away for a corner. But Völler flew to the ground upon contact, and Codesal — stuck in a poor viewing position, with Völler between him and the ball — pointed to the penalty spot.

There was nothing subtle or short about the Argentine furor this time. Maradona scolded Codesal by wagging a finger in the referee's face, and Pedro Troglio's vehemence drew a yellow card.

Unfortunately, West Germany had resorted to faking and diving. Klinsmann earlier had added melodramatic kicks and twists to Monzón's foul. Völler's reaction to Sensini's tackle was an arms–out swan dive.

Still, Goycochea had saved four penalty kicks in shootouts during the tournament, so a goal was by no means assured. He guessed the right direction this time, too, but Brehme's sharp shot eluded his right hand and nicked the base of the post before settling into the net.

Justice had been served, but it was a most unsatisfying justice. The taste soured further a few minutes later, when Codesal sent off Dezotti for clotheslining Kohler, who'd picked up the ball after Maradona had been called for a hand ball. Dezotti thought Kohler was stalling, but all he'd done was to retrieve the ball booted away after the whistle. West Germany put the ball in play, Klinsmann volleyed high on a counter–attack and the final whistle came a few minutes later.

Argentine players and officials poured onto the field to castigate Codesal, and it took several minutes before they could be calmed down enough to start the award proceedings. The crowd whistled harshly when Maradona's tearful face showed on the large viewing screen; he left abruptly, refusing to shake hands with FIFA President João Havelange and storming off before West Germany received its medals and the trophy. To their credit, his teammates stayed to applaud the champions as fireworks lit up the Olympic Stadium. ∎

Ridge Mahoney

LUCKY BREAKS

Heroes at home, villains everywhere else. Not a new situation for Argentina's national team, welcomed as conquering warriors upon their return home after losing the 1990 World Cup final to West Germany. Reaction elsewhere to their sterile play and the outrageous denunciations of Diego Maradona ranged from scolding to hostile.

Four years ago, Maradona swept Argentina to the world championship in Mexico by dazzling opponents and observers. There he displayed both the panache and controversy that have become his trademarks; against England in the quarterfinals, he scored one of the most brilliant goals in history on a solo run, five minutes after punching in one of the most insidious.

Maradona's most brilliant moment in Italia '90 set up the blonde blur Claudio Caniggia for the only goal against Brazil in the second round; no country has more Brazilian scalps than Argentina's 29.

Brazil may enjoy the romantic's adoration, but soccer on the South American continent began in Argentina. Its first club was founded in 1867 in Buenos Aires, and by 1905, dozens more had sprung in the wake of millions of European immigrants, especially Italians.

Argentina reached the final of the first World Cup, losing to host Uruguay 4–2 in 1930. Four years later, 1930 team members Raimundo Orsi and Luisito Monti played for Italy in the World Cup as *oriundi*, foreigners of Italian extraction. Such poaching and internal strife hampered Argentina's World Cup efforts for decades.

In modern times, though, Argentina has been a soccer stalwart winning the 1978 World Cup, which it hosted, and then following that eight years later with its second title in Mexico City. ∎

Ridge Mahoney

RIGHT / *Has any team ever led a more charmed existence than Argentina at World Cup 1990? When star goalie Nery Pumpido was injured early in the tournament . . .*

(inset) / *. . . Argentina was forced to turn to relatively untested Sergio Goycochea. And, as Goycochea illustrates, the defending champions also advanced on a wing — and a prayer. Though frequently outplayed by its opponents, Argentina still won, someway, somehow. Soccer purists didn't like it, and soccer fans didn't like them, but it worked.* David Jacobs / Action Images

And from here, where will Jürgen Klinsmann and West Germany soar to next? Can they defend their title in the United States in 1994? The thought of already powerful West Germany combining with East Germany to form a team from united Deutschland will give other countries plenty to work on, and worry about, until then. Daniel Motz / MOTZSPORTS

While the month-long World Cup drama unfolded in stadiums throughout Italy, that nation (and many others) screeched to a virtual halt at gametime . . .
David Jacobs / Action Images

LEFT / *. . . as the matches became part of the evening's menu for this family in Naples . . .* Luca Musella / AC

BELOW / *. . . made the pump go suddenly quiet at a Naples petrol station . . .*
Luca Musella / AC

ABOVE / . . . allowed customers to momentarily forget their hunger at a "sausage box" in Milan . . . Silva / AC

LEFT / . . . and stopped dead the shopping at the Galleria in Milan. Massimo Siragusa / AC

Hello, USA!

T he scoreboard in Rome's Stadio Olimpico said it all as the 1990 World Cup festivities came to a close:

**Ciao, Italia ´90
Hello, USA 1994**

The United States now holds center stage as host to the XVth FIFA World Cup, which will take place in as many as 12 venues around America in June and July 1994.

When the United States Soccer Federation was designated to host the 1994 tournament on July 4, 1988, a hectic chain of events was set in motion. The project has been aided from the start by an enormous outpouring of public and civic support for the World Cup.

When the World Cup ´94 Organizing Committee, the group established by the Federation to manage the herculean task, set out to determine where the games would be held, over 30 U.S. communities stepped forward, each with its own brand of remarkable fervor which soccer unleashes. The final choice of venues (a decision ultimately made by FIFA, soccer's world governing body) will be a difficult one.

Plans call for the venues to be announced in mid-1991 and the actual allocation of games to be made public later that year.

The 1990 tournament, attended by over 200 venue community leaders and nearly 200 U.S. media, futher fueled World Cup fever. From the opening ceremonies to the trophy presentation to West Germany's Lothar Matthäus, the U.S. contingent observed the tournament at close range in preparation for 1994, when the entire world will truly say, "Hello, USA." ■

RIGHT / *In Italy, American flags were waved, worn and even painted on faces. The U.S. now has its sights set on 1994, when it will proudly host the World Cup and give the world a chance to see how far the game has come in the United States.* Keyvan Antonio Heydari

statistics

 URUGUAY 1930

GROUP 1

France–Mexico	4–1					
Argentina–France	1–0					
Chile–Mexico	3–0					
Chile–France	1–0					
Argentina–Mexico	6–3					
Argentina–Chile	3–1					

	P	G	W	D	L	F	A
Argentina	6	3	3	0	0	10	4
Chile	4	3	2	0	1	5	3
France	2	3	1	0	2	4	3
Mexico	0	3	0	0	3	4	13

GROUP 2

Yugoslavia–Brazil	2–1
Yugoslavia–Bolivia	4–0
Brazil–Bolivia	4–0

	P	G	W	D	L	F	A
Yugoslavia	4	2	2	0	0	6	1
Brazil	2	2	1	0	1	5	2
Bolivia	0	2	0	0	2	0	8

GROUP 3

Romania–Peru	3–1
Uruguay–Peru	1–0
Uruguay–Romania	4–0

	P	G	W	D	L	F	A
Uruguay	4	2	2	0	0	5	0
Romania	2	2	1	0	1	3	5
Peru	0	2	0	0	2	1	4

GROUP 4

USA–Belgium	3–0
USA–Paraguay	3–0
Paraguay–Belgium	1–0

	P	G	W	D	L	F	A
USA	4	2	2	0	0	6	0
Paraguay	2	2	1	0	1	1	3
Belgium	0	2	0	0	2	0	4

SEMIFINALS

Argentina–USA	6–1
Uruguay–Yugoslavia	6–1

FINAL

Uruguay–Argentina 4–2

Montevideo, 30 July 1930

Uruguay: Ballesteros, Nasazzi, Mascheroni, Andrade, Fernandez, Gestido, Dorado, Scarone, Castro, Cea, Iriarte

Argentina: Botasso, Della Torre, Paternoster, J. Evaristo, Monti, Suarez, Peucelle, Varallo, Stabile, Ferreira, M. Evaristo

Scorers: Dorado, Cea, Iriarte, Castro; Peucelle, Stabile

 ITALY 1934

FIRST ROUND

Italy–United States	7–1	
Spain–Brazil	3–1	
Hungary–Egypt	4–2	
Austria–France	3–2	(after extra time)
Germany–Belgium	5–2	
Sweden–Argentina	3–2	
Switzerland–Holland	3–2	
Czechoslovakia–Romania	2–1	

SECOND ROUND

Italy–Spain	1–1 [1–0]
Austria–Hungary	2–1
Germany–Sweden	2–1
Czechoslovakia–Switzerland	3–2

SEMIFINALS

Italy–Austria	1–0
Czechoslovakia–Germany	3–1

THIRD PLACE MATCH

Germany–Austria	3–2 *Naples*

FINAL

Italy–Czechoslovakia 2–1 (after extra time)

Rome, 10 June 1934

Italy: Combi, Monzeglio, Allemandi, Ferraris, Monti, Bertolini, Guaita, Meazza, Schiavio, Ferrari, Orsi

Czechoslovakia: Planicka, Zenisek, Ctyroky, Kostalek, Cambal, Krcil, Junek, Svoboda, Sobotka, Nejedly, Puc

Scorers: Orsi, Schiavio; Puc

 FRANCE 1938

FIRST ROUND

Italy–Norway	2–1	(after extra time)
France–Belgium	3–1	
Czechoslovakia–Holland	3–0	(after extra time)
Brazil–Poland	6–5	
Cuba–Romania	3–1	[2–1]
Switzerland–Germany	1–1	[4–2]
Hungary–Dutch East Indies	6–0	

(Sweden received bye)

SECOND ROUND

Italy–France	3–1
Brazil–Czechoslovakia	1–1 [2–1]
Sweden–Cuba	8–0
Hungary–Switzerland	2–0

SEMIFINALS

Italy–Brazil	2–1
Hungary–Sweden	5–1

THIRD PLACE MATCH

Brazil–Sweden	4–2	
	Bordeaux	

FINAL

Italy–Hungary 4–2

Paris, 19 June 1938

Italy: Olivieri, Foni, Rava, Serantoni, Andreolo, Locatelli, Biavati, Meazza, Piola, Ferrari, Colaussi

Hungary: Szabo, Polgar, Biro, Szalay, Szucs, Lazar, Sas, Vincze, Sarosi, Szengeller, Titkos

Scorers: Colaussi 2, Piola 2; Titkos, Sarosi

 BRAZIL 1950

GROUP 1

Brazil–Mexico	4–0
Yugoslavia–Switzerland	3–0
Yugoslavia–Mexico	4–1
Brazil–Switzerland	2–2
Brazil–Yugoslavia	2–0
Switzerland–Mexico	2–0

	P	G	W	D	L	F	A
Brazil	5	3	2	1	0	8	2
Yugoslavia	4	3	2	0	1	7	3
Switzerland	3	3	1	1	1	4	6
Mexico	0	3	0	0	3	2	10

GROUP 2

Spain–United States	3–1
England–Chile	2–0
United States–England	1–0
Spain–Chile	2–0
Spain–England	1–0
Chile–United States	5–2

	P	G	W	D	L	F	A
Spain	6	3	3	0	0	6	1
England	2	3	1	0	2	2	2
Chile	2	3	1	0	2	5	6
United States	2	3	1	0	2	4	8

GROUP 3

Sweden–Italy	3–2
Sweden–Paraguay	2–2
Italy–Paraguay	2–0

	P	G	W	D	L	F	A
Sweden	3	2	1	1	0	5	4
Italy	2	2	1	0	1	4	3
Paraguay	1	2	0	1	1	2	4

GROUP 4

Uruguay–Bolivia	8–0

FINAL POOL

Uruguay–Spain	2–2
Brazil–Sweden	7–1
Uruguay–Sweden	3–2
Brazil–Spain	6–1
Sweden–Spain	3–1
Uruguay–Brazil	2–1

	P	G	W	D	L	F	A
Uruguay	5	3	2	1	0	7	5
Brazil	4	3	2	0	1	14	4
Sweden	2	3	1	0	2	6	11
Spain	1	3	0	1	2	4	11

Uruguay: Maspoli, Gonzales, Tejera, Gambetta, Varela, Andrade, Ghiggia, Perez, Miguez, Schiaffino, Moran

Brazil: Barbosa, Augusto, Juvenal, Bauer, Danilo, Bigode, Friaca, Zizinho, Ademir, Jair, Chico

Scorers: Schiaffino, Ghiggia; Friaca

 SWITZERLAND 1954

GROUP 1

Yugoslavia–France	1–0
Brazil–Mexico	5–0
France–Mexico	3–2
Brazil–Yugoslavia	1–1 (after extra time)

	P	G	W	D	L	F	A
Brazil	3	2	1	1	0	6	1
Yugoslavia	3	2	1	1	0	2	1
France	2	2	1	0	1	3	3
Mexico	0	2	0	0	2	2	8

GROUP 2

Hungary–South Korea	9–0
West Germany–Turkey	4–1
Hungary–West Germany	8–3
Turkey–South Korea	7–0

	P	G	W	D	L	F	A
Hungary	4	2	2	0	0	17	3
Turkey	2	2	1	0	1	8	4
West Germany	2	2	1	0	1	7	9
South Korea	0	2	0	0	2	0	16

Play–off: W. Germany–Turkey 7–2

GROUP 3

Austria–Scotland	1–0
Uruguay–Czechoslovakia	2–0
Austria–Czechoslovakia	5–0
Uruguay–Scotland	7–0

	P	G	W	D	L	F	A
Uruguay	4	2	2	0	0	9	0
Austria	4	2	2	0	0	6	0
Czechoslovakia	0	2	0	0	2	0	7
Scotland	0	2	0	0	2	0	8

GROUP 4

England–Belgium	4–4 (after extra time)
England–Switzerland	2–0
Switzerland–Italy	2–1
Italy–Belgium	4–1

	P	G	W	D	L	F	A
England	3	2	1	1	0	6	4
Italy	2	2	1	0	1	5	3
Switzerland	2	2	1	0	1	2	3
Belgium	1	2	0	1	1	5	8

Play–off: Switzerland–Italy 4–1

QUARTERFINALS

West Germany–Yugoslavia	2–0
Austria–Switzerland	7–5
Uruguay–England	4–2
Hungary–Brazil	4–2

SEMIFINALS

West Germany–Austria	6–1
Hungary–Uruguay	4–2

THIRD PLACE MATCH

Austria–Uruguay	3–1 *Zurich*

FINAL

W. Germany–Hungary 3–2

Berne, 4 July 1954

West Germany: Turek, Posipal, Kohlmeyer, Eckel, Liebrich, Mai, Rahn, Morlock, O. Walter, F. Walter, Schaefer

Hungary: Grosics, Buzansky, Lantos, Bozsik, Lorant, Zakarias, Czibor, Kocsis, Hidegkuti, Puskás, Toth

Scorers: Morlock, Rahn 2; Puskás, Czibor

 SWEDEN 1958

GROUP 1

West Germany–Argentina	3–1
N. Ireland–Czechoslovakia	1–0
W. Germany–Czechoslovakia	2–2
Argentina–N. Ireland	3–1
West Germany–N. Ireland	2–2
Czechoslovakia–Argentina	6–1

	P	G	W	D	L	F	A
West Germany	4	3	1	2	0	7	5
Czechoslovakia	3	3	1	1	1	8	4
N. Ireland	3	3	1	1	1	4	5
Argentina	2	3	1	0	2	5	10

Play–off: N. Ireland–Czechoslovakia 2–1
(after extra time)

GROUP 2

France–Paraguay	7–3
Yugoslavia–Scotland	1–1
Yugoslavia–France	3–2
Paraguay–Scotland	3–2
France–Scotland	2–1
Yugoslavia–Paraguay	3–3

	P	G	W	D	L	F	A
France	4	3	2	0	1	11	7
Yugoslavia	4	3	1	2	0	7	6
Paraguay	3	3	1	1	1	9	12
Scotland	1	3	0	1	2	4	6

GROUP 3

Sweden–Mexico	3–0
Hungary–Wales	1–1
Wales–Mexico	1–1
Sweden–Hungary	2–1
Hungary–Mexico	4–0
Sweden–Wales	0–0

	P	G	W	D	L	F	A
Sweden	5	3	2	1	0	5	1
Hungary	3	3	1	1	1	6	3
Wales	3	3	0	3	0	2	2
Mexico	1	3	0	1	2	1	8

Play–off: Wales–Hungary 2–1

GROUP 4

England–USSR	2–2
Brazil–Austria	3–0
Brazil–England	0–0
USSR–Austria	2–0
Brazil–USSR	2–0
England–Austria	2–2

	P	G	W	D	L	F	A
Brazil	5	3	2	1	0	5	0
England	3	3	0	3	0	4	4
USSR	3	3	1	1	1	4	4
Austria	1	3	0	1	2	2	7

Play–off: USSR–England 1–0

QUARTERFINALS

Brazil–Wales	1–0
France–Northern Ireland	4–0
West Germany–Yugoslavia	1–0
Sweden–USSR	2–0

SEMIFINALS

Brazil–France	5–2
Sweden–West Germany	3–1

THIRD PLACE MATCH

France–West Germany	6–3 *Gothenburg*

FINAL

Brazil–Sweden 5–2

Stockholm, 29 June 1958

Brazil: Gilmar, D. Santos, N. Santos, Zito, Bellini, Orlando, Garrincha, Didi, Vavá, Pelé, Zagalo

Sweden: Svensson, Bergmark, Axbom, Börjesson, Gustavsson, Parling, Hamrin, Gren, Simonsson, Liedholm, Skoglund

Scorers: Vavá 2, Pelé 2, Zagalo; Liedholm, Simonsson

 CHILE 1962

GROUP 1

Uruguay–Colombia	2–1						
USSR–Yugoslavia	2–0						
Yugoslavia–Uruguay	3–1						
USSR–Colombia	4–4						
USSR–Uruguay	2–1						
Yugoslavia–Colombia	5–0						

	P	G	W	D	L	F	A
USSR	5	3	2	1	0	8	5
Yugoslavia	4	3	2	0	1	8	3
Uruguay	2	3	1	0	2	4	6
Colombia	1	3	0	1	2	5	11

GROUP 2

Chile–Switzerland	3–1
West Germany–Italy	0–0
Chile–Italy	2–0
West Germany–Switzerland	2–1
West Germany–Chile	2–0
Italy–Switzerland	3–0

	P	G	W	D	L	F	A
West Germany	5	3	2	1	0	4	1
Chile	4	3	2	0	1	5	3
Italy	3	3	1	1	1	3	2
Switzerland	0	3	0	0	3	2	8

GROUP 3

Brazil–Mexico	2–1
Czechoslovakia–Spain	1–0
Brazil–Czechoslovakia	0–0
Spain–Mexico	1–0
Brazil–Spain	2–1
Mexico–Czechoslovakia	3–1

	P	G	W	D	L	F	A
Brazil	5	3	2	1	0	4	1
Czechoslovakia	3	3	1	1	1	2	3
Mexico	2	3	1	0	2	3	4
Spain	2	3	1	0	2	2	3

GROUP 4

Argentina–Bulgaria	1–0
Hungary–England	2–1
England–Argentina	3–1
Hungary–Bulgaria	6–1
Hungary–Argentina	0–0
England–Bulgaria	0–0

	P	G	W	D	L	F	A
Hungary	5	3	2	1	0	8	2
England*	3	3	1	1	1	4	3
Argentina	3	3	1	1	1	2	3
Bulgaria	1	3	0	1	2	1	7

*qualified on goal difference

QUARTERFINALS

Brazil–England	3–1
Chile–USSR	2–1
Yugoslavia–West Germany	1–0
Czechoslovakia–Hungary	1–0

SEMIFINALS

Brazil–Chile	4–2
Czechoslovakia–Yugoslavia	3–1

THIRD PLACE MATCH

Chile–Yugoslavia	1–0	*Santiago*

FINAL

Brazil–Czechoslovakia   3–1

Santiago, 17 June 1962

Brazil: Gilmar, D. Santos, N. Santos, Zito, Mauro, Zozimo, Garrincha, Didi, Vavá, Amarildo, Zagalo

Czechoslovakia: Schroiff, Tichy, Novak, Pluskal, Popluhar, Masopust, Pospichal, Scherer, Kvasniak, Kadraba, Jelinek

Scorers: Amarildo, Zito, Vavá; Masopust

 ENGLAND 1966

GROUP 1

England–Uruguay	0–0
France–Mexico	1–1
Uruguay–France	2–1
England–Mexico	2–0
Uruguay–Mexico	0–0
England–France	2–0

	P	G	W	D	L	F	A
England	5	3	2	1	0	4	0
Uruguay	4	3	1	2	0	2	1
Mexico	2	3	0	2	1	1	3
France	1	3	0	1	2	2	5

GROUP 2

West Germany–Switzerland	5–0
Argentina–Spain	2–1
Spain–Switzerland	2–1
West Germany–Argentina	0–0
Argentina–Switzerland	2–0
West Germany–Spain	2–1

	P	G	W	D	L	F	A
West Germany	5	3	2	1	0	7	1
Argentina	5	3	2	1	0	4	1
Spain	2	3	1	0	2	4	5
Switzerland	0	3	0	0	3	1	9

GROUP 3

Brazil–Bulgaria	2–0
Portugal–Hungary	3–1
Hungary–Brazil	3–1
Portugal–Bulgaria	3–0
Portugal–Brazil	3–1
Hungary–Bulgaria	3–1

	P	G	W	D	L	F	A
Portugal	6	3	3	0	0	9	2
Hungary	4	3	2	0	1	7	5
Brazil	2	3	1	0	2	4	6
Bulgaria	0	3	0	0	3	1	8

GROUP 4

USSR–North Korea	3–0
Italy–Chile	2–0
Chile–North Korea	1–1
USSR–Italy	1–0
North Korea–Italy	1–0
USSR–Chile	2–1

	P	G	W	D	L	F	A
USSR	6	3	3	0	0	6	1
North Korea	3	3	1	1	1	2	4
Italy	2	3	1	0	2	2	2
Chile	1	3	0	1	2	2	5

QUARTERFINALS

England–Argentina	1–0
Portugal–North Korea	5–3
USSR–Hungary	2–1
West Germany–Uruguay	4–0

SEMIFINALS

England–Portugal	2–1
West Germany–USSR	2–1

THIRD PLACE MATCH

Portugal–USSR	2–1	*Wembley*

FINAL

England–W. Germany   4–2 (after extra time)

Wembley, 30 July 1966

England: Banks, Cohen, Wilson, Stiles, J. Charlton, Moore, Ball, Hunt, Hurst, R. Charlton, Peters

West Germany: Tilkowski, Hottges, Schnellinger, Beckenbauer, Schultz, Weber, Held, Haller, Seeler, Overath, Emmerich

Scorers: Hurst 3, Peters; Haller, Weber

 MEXICO 1970

GROUP 1

Mexico–USSR	0–0
Belgium–El Salvador	3–0
USSR–Belgium	4–1
Mexico–El Salvador	4–0
USSR–El Salvador	2–0
Mexico–Belgium	1–0

	P	G	W	D	L	F	A
USSR	5	3	2	1	0	6	1
Mexico	5	3	2	1	0	5	0
Belgium	2	3	1	0	2	4	5
El Salvador	0	3	0	0	3	0	9

GROUP 2

Uruguay–Israel		2–0					
Italy–Sweden		1–0					
Italy–Uruguay		0–0					
Israel–Sweden		1–1					
Sweden–Uruguay		1–0					
Italy–Israel		0–0					

	P	G	W	D	L	F	A
Italy	4	3	1	2	0	1	0
Uruguay*	3	3	1	1	1	2	1
Sweden	3	3	1	1	1	2	2
Israel	2	3	0	2	1	1	3

*qualified on goal difference

GROUP 3

England–Romania		1–0
Brazil–Czechoslovakia		4–1
Romania–Czechoslovakia		2–1
Brazil–England		1–0
Brazil–Romania		3–2
England–Czechoslovakia		1–0

	P	G	W	D	L	F	A
Brazil	6	3	3	0	0	8	3
England	4	3	2	0	1	2	1
Romania	2	3	1	0	2	4	5
Czechoslovakia	0	3	0	0	3	2	7

GROUP 4

Peru–Bulgaria		3–2
West Germany–Morocco		2–1
Peru–Morocco		3–0
West Germany–Bulgaria		5–2
West Germany–Peru		3–1
Bulgaria–Morocco		1–1

	P	G	W	D	L	F	A
West Germany	6	3	3	0	0	10	4
Peru	4	3	2	0	1	7	5
Bulgaria	1	3	0	1	2	5	9
Morocco	1	3	0	1	2	2	6

QUARTERFINALS

Brazil–Peru	4–2	
Uruguay–USSR	1–0	
West Germany–England	3–2	(after extra time)
Italy–Mexico	4–1	

SEMIFINALS

Brazil–Uruguay	3–1	
Italy–West Germany	4–3	(after extra time)

THIRD PLACE MATCH

West Germany–Uruguay	1–0	*Mexico City*

FINAL

Brazil–Italy	4–1

Mexico City, 21 June 1970

Brazil: Felix, Carlos Alberto, Brito, Wilson Piazza, Everaldo, Clodoaldo, Gerson, Jairzinho, Tostão, Pelé, Rivelino

Italy: Albertosi, Burgnich, Facchetti, Cera, Rosato, Bertini (Juliano), Domenghini, Mazzola, Boninsegna (Rivera), De Sisti, Riva

Scorers: Pelé, Gerson, Jairzinho, Carlos Alberto; Boninsegna

 W. GERMANY 1974

GROUP 1

West Germany–Chile	1–0
East Germany–Australia	2–0
West Germany–Australia	3–0
East Germany–Chile	1–1
E. Germany–W. Germany	1–0
Chile–Australia	0–0

	P	G	W	D	L	F	A
East Germany	5	3	2	1	0	4	1
West Germany	4	3	2	0	1	4	1
Chile	2	3	0	2	1	1	2
Australia	1	3	0	1	2	0	5

GROUP 2

Brazil–Yugoslavia	0–0
Scotland–Zaire	2–0
Brazil–Scotland	0–0
Yugoslavia–Zaire	9–0
Yugoslavia–Scotland	1–1
Brazil–Zaire	3–0

	P	G	W	D	L	F	A
Yugoslavia*	4	3	1	2	0	10	1
Brazil*	4	3	1	2	0	3	0
Scotland	4	3	1	2	0	3	1
Zaire	0	3	0	0	3	0	14

*qualified on goal difference

GROUP 3

Holland–Uruguay	2–0
Sweden–Bulgaria	0–0
Holland–Sweden	0–0
Bulgaria–Uruguay	1–1
Holland–Bulgaria	4–1
Sweden–Uruguay	3–0

	P	G	W	D	L	F	A
Holland	5	3	2	1	0	6	1
Sweden	4	3	1	2	0	3	0
Bulgaria	2	3	0	2	1	2	5
Uruguay	1	3	0	1	2	1	6

GROUP 4

Italy–Haiti	3–1
Poland–Argentina	3–2
Argentina–Italy	1–1
Poland–Haiti	7–0
Argentina–Haiti	4–1
Poland–Italy	2–1

	P	G	W	D	L	F	A
Poland	6	3	3	0	0	12	3
Argentina*	3	3	1	1	1	7	5
Italy	3	3	1	1	1	5	4
Haiti	0	3	0	0	3	2	14

*qualified on goal difference

GROUP A

Holland–Argentina	4–0
Brazil–East Germany	1–0
Holland–East Germany	2–0
Brazil–Argentina	2–1
Holland–Brazil	2–0
East Germany–Argentina	1–1

	P	G	W	D	L	F	A
Holland	6	3	3	0	0	8	0
Brazil	4	3	2	0	1	3	3
East Germany	1	3	0	1	2	1	4
Argentina	1	3	0	1	2	2	7

GROUP B

West Germany–Yugoslavia	2–0
Poland–Sweden	1–0
Poland–Yugoslavia	2–1
West Germany–Sweden	4–2
Sweden–Yugoslavia	2–1
West Germany–Poland	1–0

	P	G	W	D	L	F	A
West Germany	6	3	3	0	0	7	2
Poland	4	3	2	0	1	3	2
Sweden	2	3	1	0	2	4	6
Yugoslavia	0	3	0	0	3	2	6

THIRD PLACE MATCH

Poland–Brazil	1–0	*Munich*

FINAL

West Germany–Holland	2–1

Munich, 7 July 1974

West Germany: Maier, Vogts, Schwarzenbeck, Beckenbauer, Breitner, Bonhof, Hoeness, Grabowski, Müller, Overath, Holzenbein

Holland: Jongbloed, Suurbier, Rijsbergen (De Jong), Haan, Krol, Jansen, Van Hanegem, Neeskens, Rep, Cruyff, Rensenbrink (R Van der Kerkhof)

Scorers: Breitner (pen), Müller; Neeskens (pen)

 ARGENTINA 1978

GROUP 1

Italy–France	2–1
Argentina–Hungary	2–1
Italy–Hungary	3–1
Argentina–France	2–1
France–Hungary	3–1
Italy–Argentina	1–0

	P	G	W	D	L	F	A
Italy	6	3	3	0	0	6	2
Argentina	4	3	2	0	1	4	3
France	2	3	1	0	2	5	5
Hungary	0	3	0	0	3	3	8